7 STEPS TO SKIPPERING A YACHT

RICHARD THOMAS

RYA YachtMaster (Ocean)

Copyright © 2015 Richard Thomas

Published by Spider Communication Limited
Registered in England no: 5676656
71B St Thomas Street, Wells, Somerset BA5 2UY, United Kingdom

Cover Photograph: Hallberg-Rassy 412
Photo: Hallberg-Rassy/Peter Szamer

All rights reserved.

ISBN: **1507608098**
ISBN-13: **978-1507608098**

ABOUT THE SERIES

This book is the second in a series that covers every aspect of owning and sailing a yacht. Visit www.7stepbooks.com to join our mailing list and get more information about the other books in the series as they are published. Other books in the series:

7 Steps to Buying a Yacht
This book could save you a lot of money by helping you avoid buying the wrong yacht. We'll go through all the things you need to think about before getting out your cheque book.

It will help you to ask all the right questions before you buy. Questions like: What kind of sailing do you want to do? What are the hidden costs that will affect your budget? What size of Yacht will suit you best? What Hull shape and build material will suit your sailing? What kind of sail plan would work for you? What equipment do you want to fit?

There's a fairly comprehensive check list that'll help you when you view a potential yacht, and you can make notes for the surveyor. You'll learn how to check for unpaid bills and outstanding loans on the yacht, and how to avoid getting stung when you make the purchase.

7 Steps to Crewing a Yacht
Stepping on board a sailing yacht for the first time can be both exciting and scary. The third book in the series will take you through all the initial challenges you're likely to meet.

From knowing what to take with you (and what to leave behind), what all the ropes and levers actually do, how to live comfortably on board, coping with sea sickness and fear, to the all important understanding of how to get on with the Skipper and your fellow crew members.

If you're crewing on a yacht for the first time, this book will give you a great head start. It might even save your life!

CONTENTS

	Acknowledgments	i
1	Introduction	1
2	Step One - Being in Command	3
3	Step Two - Knowing the Rules	7
4	Step Three - Knowing the Passage	12
5	Step Four - Knowing your Crew	26
6	Step Five - Knowing your Sailing Skills	43
7	Step Six - Knowing your Yacht	60
8	Step Seven - Knowing your Resources	74
9	Post Script	82
10	Appendix 1 - Crew Invitation Form	83
11	Appendix 2 - Example of Standing Orders	89

ACKNOWLEDGMENTS

I am grateful to all those yacht owners who invited YachtMovers (http://www.yachtmovers.co.uk) to deliver their yachts, giving me unparalleled experience of sailing all shapes and sizes of yachts in different parts of the world, and learning from them those things that can never be learned from a course or a book.

I am grateful to Glenn Smallcombe of Quantum Sailing, an excellent YachtMaster Instructor and sailing companion, whose patience and professionalism has been an inspiration to many.
His comments have been invaluable.

My wife, Jane, has played her part too. Despite being pathologically averse to sailing, after thirty years of marriage she did come out to sail with me in the Saronic. It was a pity the weather wasn't better.

Finally, I fully acknowledge the equality of sex and gender. But continually writing 'he or she', and varying it as 'she or he' in order to make that equality visible, is very tiring on both the reader and the writer. So I have adopted the age-old convention of writing 'he' and meaning 'he or she' with no intimation that either sex or gender is superior to the other when it comes to skippering a yacht.

Being safely 'in command' is what matters.

INTRODUCTION

The aim of this book is to help you grow as a safe and reliable skipper of a sea-going cruising yacht.

There is very little in life more satisfying than skippering a yacht across a bit of water to a new port. It doesn't matter much whether it's five miles or five thousand. Getting there is always an adventure, and arrival is always deeply satisfying.

But there's a lot more to skippering a yacht than knowing how to sail. In fact, most of the skills you'll need are in managing the crew rather than the yacht.

So I've broken this book down into a number of areas of 'knowing' that a safe and competent skipper will need to master. They're all necessary, and trying to decide which to put first wasn't easy. But essentially, skippering is about being 'in command'. So this comes first, along with knowing the essential 'rules of the road'.

However, even if you've mastered everything else, without a thorough understanding of the passage you're about to make you won't be either safe or competent. So I've continued with a section on 'Knowing the passage'. We'll work together through a voyage from the earliest planning stage to the point where you've safely tied up alongside in your destination port, and the crew have insisted you join them ashore for a celebration beer and some food because they 'thoroughly enjoyed' it, even though it presented some significant challenges.

And then, in the following sections, we'll look at the kind of decisions you'll need to make, and what factors will help you make them.

From sailing skills to passage planning and navigation, from crew selection and watch keeping options to understanding the constraints of your yacht. We'll look at victualing and cooking arrangement, sea berths and crew comforts. There's a short section on heavy weather, and we'll look at how to make, and equally important, how to communicate difficult decisions. Do you need to turn back? Do you need to change your plans? Do you need to call for help?

These kinds of decisions are difficult. They come with experience, and if you don't have experience the next best thing is to read about other people's decisions and how they worked (or didn't work).

I freely admit that the Seven Steps approach is a device to help guide you through the process of learning. There's a lot to learn. But there's an old joke that asks: How do you eat an elephant? Answer: one step at a time!

STEP ONE - BEING IN COMMAND

Many thousands of people take up yachting as a leisure activity, and a good percentage of them will do an RYA course or the equivalent to learn the basic skills. Many will go on to skipper their own yacht, or to skipper a charter holiday. But knowing how to plot a course or read a chart won't automatically turn them into good, safe skippers.

As a delivery skipper and RYA Instructor, I've sailed with many technically competent yachtsmen and women who know the theory, but whose understanding and experience of 'command' and how to get the best from their crew and their yacht is sorely lacking.

So this isn't a 'get you through the Yacht Master Exam' type book because it doesn't deal with any of the technical skills needed. There are plenty of those books already. What it does try to do is to pass on some of the things that an RYA course can't teach in the few short hours allowed for the technical syllabus.

Is he safe?

Or she. Some of the best skippers I know are women. Whatever your age, or your gender, it's the question that most crew (and their families) have at the back of their minds, if not at the front. It's the question that the RNLI ask of you, simply by being there. They'd rather not launch because of your actions.

And most examiners I know ask themselves the same, simple, basic question: 'Is this candidate safe to sail with?'

The answer comes in two parts. Does he or she have the necessary skills, and does he or she have an attitude or approach to the task that will make him or her a safe and competent skipper?

This book deals with the second of those two questions by looking at seven areas of 'knowing' that a good, safe skipper will pay attention to. There isn't one right answer to many of these, and each skipper will have his or her own approach. But learning from others, even if you end up disagreeing or doing things differently, is a great place to start.

In Command

Those two words are what it's all about.

It's not about the freedom to issue orders like confetti, or to do what you like. And it's certainly not about shouting at the crew. It's about making the right decisions at the right time. And it's about taking responsibility.

Being in command of a sailing yacht at sea is one of the greatest pleasures I know. There's nothing quite like the feel of the wind on your face, the comforting motion of the sea and the wide-open spaces to relax and nurture you. Those who have little experience of the deep oceans may think that it's a lonely place, but I've never found that. For me, the ocean is a comforting place, a place of beauty and adventure.

It can, of course, be challenging at times. And on a few occasions it can be dangerous. The sea is impersonal, and bad weather or structural problems can come from nowhere. But for most of the time, it's a wonderful place to be.

In British waters, and provided it's not a commercial passage (i.e., apart from a small contribution towards victualing costs, no one is being charged for the voyage) you don't actually need any qualifications whatsoever before you can step on board your yacht and set sail as skipper.

And long may it last. Because one of the hallmarks of a good skipper is that you don't rely on a vast array of laws and regulations to tell you how to do it. A good skipper takes full and personal responsibility for the safety and comfort of the yacht and the crew, and for every aspect of the passage at every stage, in harbour or at sea, whether or not he or she is on board at the time.

It's not about rules

We live in a society that is increasingly besotted with regulation. The excuse often given is that safety is important, and without regulation we won't be safe. This is both true and complete nonsense at the same time. Safety is hugely important, but a good skipper won't need regulations to be safe.

I've never seen a regulation that will stop a boom in the middle of an uncontrolled gybe, or a law that will prevent someone falling over the side in a force seven. There's not a law written that will help you notice a crew member who's in danger of hypothermia because he is feeling too sea sick to go below.

In fact, over-regulation actually decreases safety, because it's human nature to do the bare minimum to keep within the rules, and rules can never cover every eventuality.

Of course, there are idiots about. And for some reason, natural selection doesn't seem to have worked all that well in removing them from society. But it's having a fair crack at removing them from the sea. There have been too many fatal accidents recently where people have ignored wise warnings or set out to sea with inadequate experience and preparation. But, natural selection aside, you can't legislate or regulate a safe or competent skipper into being. It has to come from the individual. It has to be something you take seriously yourself.

It's the skipper's call...

Good skippering means undertaking the voyage in a way that brings maximum enjoyment to the crew, gets the yacht safely and expeditiously to her destination, and doesn't inconvenience or put other vessels at risk. It includes good delegation, a relaxed and confident understanding of the skills required, quiet empathy, and absolute fairness. And it requires experience.

You can't legislate for the kind of personal qualities that will deliver these. Once you start trying, you encourage a 'speed camera' mentality where the rules are obeyed when someone's checking, but completely ignored when they're not. And who's going to check at two in the morning a hundred miles or so off the coast?

There might be an argument for requiring skippers to hold the ICC (International Certificate of Competence) qualification, which would bring us into line with other European countries by showing that the skipper has achieved a basic level of yacht management skills. There have been a too many fatal accidents recently because fundamental sailing skills were missing. But more than that is over-kill.

If anything goes wrong, the responsibility remains with the skipper. If a mistake was made by a watch keeper, it's still the skipper's responsibility. If there's an engine or rig failure, it's up to the skipper to sort it. Bad weather ahead? It's the skipper's call. That's what it means to be 'In Command'.

Personal responsibility isn't just about obeying rules. In fact, it's not really about rules at all. It's about making the kind of decisions that will enhance the safety and enjoyability of the passage. You can work hard to get your Day Skipper or YachtMaster ticket, and know how to plan and execute a passage. You can study for your Ocean ticket and get all your sights right. But if your crew ends up hating you, you won't enjoy it and neither will they.

Foreseeing problems

I once asked some sailing friends what they thought made a good skipper. They agreed that 'A good skipper is one who foresees a problem and either solves or avoids it when the crew may not even know it was a problem at all'.

That sense of foresight is what lies at the heart of becoming a good skipper. It's second nature to an experienced skipper, but it requires the ability to do lots of 'what if' thinking. We'll cover this in more detail when we get to step six, 'Knowing your Yacht', but it applies in just about all situations.

A good skipper is going to have a kind of mental 'check list' of things to think about, a 'what if' mentality that foresees potential problems and thinks of ways of dealing with them well in advance.

And he or she may not have either the time or the energy to explain every 'what if' to the crew. She may simply want things done 'that way'. But there will be reasons. Some skippers have a 'touchy feely' approach and will spend a long time educating the crew about why things should be done a particular way. Others will remain distant and apparently aloof, but will still have the care of the yacht and her crew at the heart of their thinking.

Being liked - not!

Being in Command is about taking personal responsibility, and doing things that may or may not be popular with the crew. Getting them up in the middle of the night because there needs to be a safe number of crew for a sail change in deteriorating weather won't be popular. But it will be safe.

Being in Command isn't about being 'liked'. Your experience, coupled with a fair treatment of your crew, may result in your being respected. Being 'liked' isn't necessarily an outcome. In fact, being in command is essentially a lonely place to be. If you have a good, reliable first mate with whom you can share some of the thinking and decisions, it can be a great help. But the bottom line is that it's your responsibility, your decision. You can't run a yacht by committee. And you can't make decisions based on whether they make you popular with the crew.

STEP TWO - KNOWING THE RULES

Whilst you can't be a good skipper merely by following rules, there are important rules that need to be followed. And if you're a safe and responsible skipper, you'll follow them. You won't add to them, or make up your own for the sake of convenience or a supposed superior knowledge.

The Collision Regulations

For example, let's look at the International Regulations for Preventing Collisions at Sea (IRPCS), known almost universally as the 'Col Regs'. These are the 'rules of the road' for merchant and leisure craft alike, and a safe and competent skipper will not only know them all and follow them meticulously, but will have them available on board and will encourage his or her crew to learn them.

Knowing the Collision Regulations is probably the single most fundamental piece of safety knowledge for any yacht skipper. And by knowing, I don't just mean knowing that you turn to starboard in a potential head-on close encounter. Rule 2 states:

Nothing in these Rules shall exonerate any vessel, or the owner, master or crew thereof, from the consequences of any neglect to comply with these Rules or of the neglect of any precaution which may be required by the ordinary practice of seamen, or by the special circumstances of the case.

In other words, the Collision Regulations are fundamental to safe and competent seamanship. There are plenty of places where you can find a helpful version of the regulations, and one of the best self-learning tools is 'A Seaman's Guide to the Rules of the Road' by J.W.W.Ford, available on Amazon here. Or you can download the Merchant Shipping Notice published by the Maritime Coastguard Agency here.

It's one thing knowing them, but it's quite another following them, particularly if you're a small yacht facing a super tanker at sea. The temptation is to think that 'they don't apply to me' when all your instincts are simply to keep out of the way.

Stand on Vessels - an example

One of the most common mistakes made by inexperienced yacht skippers when crossing a busy shipping lane concerns the rule for "stand on" vessels. No one has 'right of way' at sea, but the rules for two vessels under power and under way are unambiguous. They clearly state which of them has to hold its course and speed (the "stand on" vessel) and which has to alter course and/or speed (the 'give way' vessel) to avoid a collision.

So imagine the following. A large container ship travelling at over twenty knots is crossing the path of a small, thirty foot yacht motoring along under power doing about four knots. The yacht has its mainsail up for stability, but is showing the motoring cone, and because of wind direction and speed there can be no doubt that it's motoring. The container ship is crossing in front of the yacht, from port to starboard, and is on what looks like a steady bearing. It is therefore the 'give way' vessel. The yacht is the 'stand on' vessel. Collision Regulation Rule 17, Action by stand-on vessel, states that

> *'Where one of two vessels is to keep out of the way the other shall keep her course and speed."*

Telling you which way to turn is good. But telling you to keep your course and speed can seem counter-intuitive. Seeing a huge container vessel heading towards you on what looks like a collision course (or even anything that might remotely be a collision course) is scary for an inexperienced skipper. Seeing the container ship bearing down on him, he might well be tempted to turn, or slow down, or push hard on the throttle to cross first. It's the natural, instinctive reaction of a pedestrian crossing a motorway. An 'oh shit' moment for the inexperienced skipper, who just wants to be anywhere but there.

But the Officer of the Watch on the container ship has most probably seen the yacht on radar a while back, plotted its closest point of approach (CPA), checked it visually a few times, and altered course by a few degrees so that he will pass astern no closer than half a mile. He may have decided that the CPA shows that he isn't on a collision course at all, and will pass safely ahead. He will know that his vessel is the 'give way' vessel. He will have made sure that the lookout is tracking the yacht visually. He's done it hundreds of times before. That calculation, probably performed by the software on the bridge of the container ship and checked by the Officer of the Watch, will be based on the assumption (a) that the yacht skipper will know the rules of the road, and (b) that he will follow them.

In other words, that he will 'keep his course and speed'.

However, the inexperienced yacht skipper panics. He slows down, or maybe even turns 180 degrees to get out of the way. Either action could put him slap in the path of the container ship. Alarms go off on the bridge of the container ship as the electronically calculated and constantly monitored CPA closes to less than 100 yards. The Officer of the Watch follows his standing orders and calls the Captain. The Captain, uncertain of the yacht's movements, now orders a crash stop. But he can't slow down in time, and a close quarters situation rapidly develops.

That's how accidents happen

At least one has happened almost exactly like that, and it's why a 'stand on' vessel should hold its course and speed. Of course, the skipper of a 'stand on' yacht should continue to check the CPA himself as best he can to make sure that a close quarters situation doesn't develop. If the bearing remains steady, then there is a risk of collision, and under the rules the yacht skipper will need to take action if it does. But there's always the VHF radio, and he can call the bridge of the ship if he's in any doubt. If the rules say 'hold your course and speed', that's exactly what you do unless it's clear that the other ship isn't taking sufficient action.

I've had to tell a number of aspiring skippers to keep their course and speed in such circumstances. It's counter intuitive, particularly when commercial pressure on large vessels means that they waste as little fuel as possible by making only small course changes to avoid close quarters situations. It isn't always obvious to a yacht when a large vessel makes a small course correction. AIS (the Automatic Identification System fitted to all large commercial vessels which broadcasts their course and speed, amongst other things) can help a lot here by showing you that the vessel has changed course by a few degrees, and by giving you a calculated CPA, but experience, and holding your nerve when crossing the path of a huge tanker, is what counts.

Personal responsibility and experience

One of the first tests of good skippering is making sure that you have the necessary skills and experience for the passage you're going to undertake. Not because the law requires it (which, in British waters, it doesn't), but because you know that unless you have those skills and that experience, you could be putting your crew, your yacht and yourself at risk. And because you're following the single most important rule of being a good skipper - you're taking personal responsibility.

Of course, one of the ingredients is experience. You won't get that out of a book, and you won't get it second-hand from others. It comes with time, through learning from mistakes, and with fear - yes, I do mean fear – fear that grips your stomach at one in the morning on a dark, wet night when you haven't checked the weather forecast properly. As they say, smooth seas never made a skilled sailor. The same fear you feel those first few times when you encounter a large vessel in a crossing position. Anyone who tells me they've never felt fear at sea is someone I'd rather not sail with.

Experience is earned, not learned. But you can get pointed in the right direction by sailing with other skippers, and by reading other people's personal experience of decision making under tough conditions.

Reading the Pilot Book

Here's another example. You're in an unexpected strong westerly blow, and the pilot book warns you that the entrance to the harbour you were heading for is dangerous in strong Westerlies. The crew are feeling tired, one is sea sick, and night is approaching. Several of the crew mention rather pointedly how much they're looking forward to being alongside. The skipper himself is feeling a trifle worried, a little tired, and at the edge of his experience.

The inexperienced skipper might well give in to pressure. He might not take the pilot book seriously, or might even not have read it. He might assume that the safest thing to do is to head for the nearest harbour at full tilt just to get out of the discomfort of the storm. So he heads for a harbour the pilot book says is dangerous in strong Westerlies. He sails across increasingly shallow water where the waves are steeper and possibly breaking, where it's impossible to cook or even sleep, aiming for a harbour entrance that could roll the yacht. He might just make it safely, but there's no guarantee. He's gambling with the lives of his crew and himself, as well as the safety of the yacht. Yachts have been rolled and lives lost by just such an action.

But the experienced skipper will brief the crew, explain the risk, and head out to deeper water where it's safer. His calm authority and experience will show. He will sail the yacht for maximum comfort, heaving to if possible, so that the cook can at least produce some warming soup. He will already have planned an alternative safe port, if there is one. If not, he will stay out until dawn, when everyone will feel more in control, and when it's easier to assess the safety of entering an unknown harbour. Meanwhile, he will take care of his seasick crew, and the reassurance of his safety briefing will help them all understand the reasons. He certainly won't approach a dangerous entrance at night in strong winds. The experienced skipper will keep his yacht and his crew safe.

Knowing national regulations

We have it fairly easy in England. As a member of the European Union, sailing to another EU country involves very little paperwork. You can leave Yarmouth on the Isle of Wight very early in the morning, sail across to Cherbourg, tie up alongside, and go for dinner in France without meeting a single official.

But each country has its own rules and regulations, and as they say, ignorance of the law is no defence. Even in the EU, regulations differ about how long you and your yacht can stay in a country, what documentation and qualifications you need, and what you can and can't bring in with you.

One example (mentioned before) is the documentary evidence needed to prove competence as a skipper. In British waters, such evidence is not required. But in most other European countries, it is. An International Certificate of Competence is almost universally recognised as sufficient - and it's just a little less demanding that the RYA Day Skipper exam.

Another example is the length of time you are allowed to stay in a country with your yacht before you have to import it. Even some EU countries are getting very picky about this, and it pays to know the national regulations and stick to them.

There's an extremely useful website called Noonsite.com that has all the important information to hand for each country in the world, together with ports of entry. All the information is completely free, but that doesn't mean that it's not accurate. This is how it describes itself:

> *Noonsite began in 2000 as a culmination of Jimmy Cornell's books (World Cruising Handbook and World Cruising Routes) and his work on the global cruising scene for the last quarter of a century. It has since grown extensively, in the main thanks to constant updates and cruising reports from sailors using the site and regular contributions from our regional editors.*
>
> *Noonsite aims to provide a one-stop website featuring essential information on all matters of interest to sailors planning an offshore voyage anywhere in the world, whether already underway or still in the preparatory stages.*

Noonsite is perhaps one of the most useful sailing websites anywhere. The best way to experience it is to look up a country you plan on visiting to see the detail and quality of the information included there. If I am planning a visit to any country, EU or otherwise, Noonsite is a 'must read' for that country as part of my planning.

STEP THREE - KNOWING THE PASSAGE

To help you think about some of the issues faced by the skipper of an ocean going yacht, we're going to plan an imaginary voyage from Gosport on the South Coast of England to Gibraltar. We'll be using a 45' yacht big enough to accommodate eight people in comfort, which will give us a good number of options for watch keeping. It will also increase our planning speed from a very cautious five knots to a possible six.

The advantage of choosing this length of passage is that it can cover everything from day and weekend sailing as you meet the crew and position the yacht for departure, to a Biscay crossing and a long offshore passage. It will involve 'going foreign' to both EU and non EU countries, and can touch on just about everything you might need to know about skippering a Sailing Yacht at sea.

And of course, throughout this book I'll be doing it 'my way'. But that doesn't mean that it's the only way, or even the only right way. Very often when it comes to the different styles of command there isn't a single 'right answer'. If you disagree with the way I suggest doing things, that's fine. You're the skipper. But the mark of a good skipper is that they never stop learning from others. So even if you decide to do things differently, or disagree with the way I suggest running a yacht, I hope that what I write will help you to define and understand your own leadership style better, and will help make you a better skipper.

Start planning early

Quite often, the planning will start months before the actual passage, and the anticipation of each stage of the passage can be one sailing's greatest pleasures. Even when you're not making notes, you may well be turning the options over in your mind. In the cold and damp of an English winter, it can be a great pleasure to pull the Pilot book off the shelf and study up on all the possible ports you might visit on the way, as well as the tricky bits of the passage.

And it's not just for anticipation, either. Taking time to mull over the passage and the various options can make things a lot easier to manage when you get stuck into the detail. And at two in the morning on a dark and very stormy night, when things begin to get difficult, that familiarity with the passage can make the difference between calm reassurance and an air of suppressed panic.

Planning the route

With today's Internet technology, there are some great tools available to you for this first part of the planning process. Google Earth is invaluable for the first stages of passage planning. In fact, whenever I get asked to plan a voyage, it's usually where I go first.

The first thing you want to know is roughly how long the passage is in nautical miles and what the route options are. From this you can make a very rough estimate of the time scale for the passage.

Gosport to Gibraltar

Let's look at the overview for a passage from Gosport to Gibraltar.

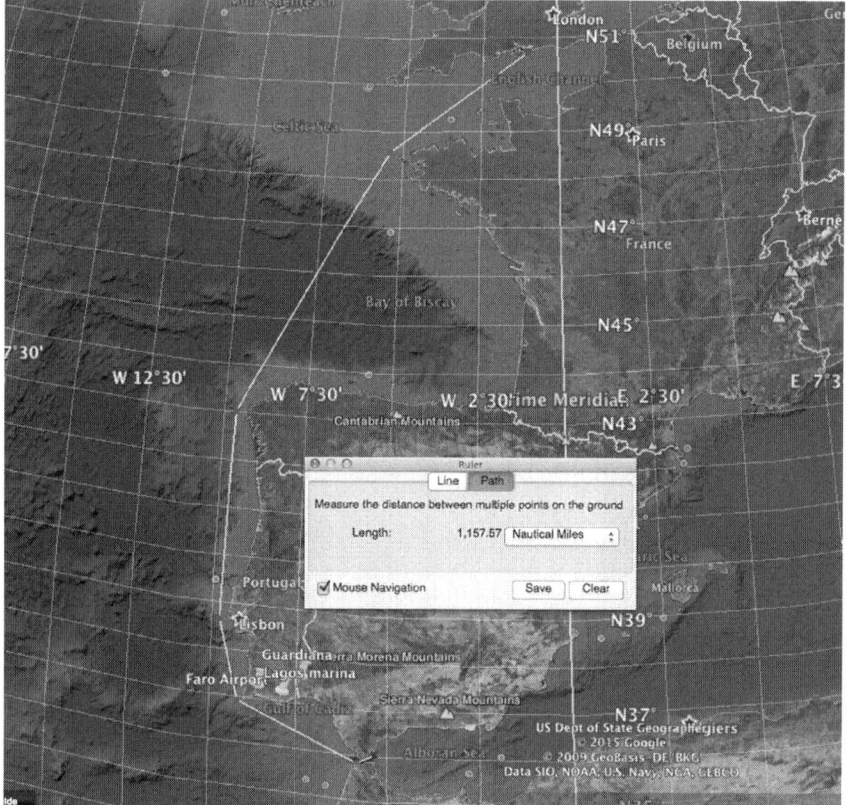

Google Earth gives you an initial passage outline

A quick visit to Google Earth tells you that the shortest route is going to be about 1,140 nautical miles.

That's going outside Ushant (which is easier than taking the inshore route), but hugging the coast where you can, and heading off directly from Gosport. At a rough planning speed of five knots, and with favourable winds, it's going to take you nine and a half days non-stop. Or with our faster 45' yacht and some good winds, around eight days non-stop.

But unless you have exceptional weather, a fully trained crew, a tested and trusted yacht, and you're in a great hurry, you're not going to go non-stop. You'll need at least one shake-down cruise first. A short initial passage down to the west of England, to Plymouth, Dartmouth or even Falmouth, can give you a greater understanding of your yacht and your crew, as well as the time to fix any issues that present themselves, either with the crew or with the yacht.

And your Biscay passage may well take you a little further west than the direct route shows, because the weather and sea state may be a little more comfortable if you have a slightly more southerly wind angle. But it's only an option; you'll have to make those kinds of decisions when you have a reliable weather forecast.

Plan for changes

Drawing a line on a chart showing the most direct route is one thing; being able to follow it with adverse winds, close hauled or from a different departure point is another. It's usually the first casualty of the passage plan. The one key bit of data you're going to need in order to finalise the planning is the likely wind direction and strength, and you won't get that for certain until you're about to depart - and even then, it's only a forecast, not a certainty.

Flexibility is the skipper's friend. Which is why spending time with the pilot book and the charts, and getting a good mental map of the many different possibilities presented by the passage, is a good thing to do.

But even with the weather and other issues to factor in nearer the time, you can still plan for an 'ideal' route, recognising that you may need to make adjustments later on.

A three stage passage

Going direct is still an option, but an unlikely one. A much better plan might be to break the passage into three sections. The first leg might be to day sail to a departure point in the West of England or even the Channel Islands or North West France. This allows you to do several things.

Firstly, you are positioning the yacht for the next section of the passage, which is the Biscay crossing with landfall in northern Spain at La Corunna, Camarinas, or one of the Rias such as Vigo or Bayonne. And whilst at first it might not seem worth the extra hassle in order to reduce the second leg by a mere hundred miles or so, you're gaining several big advantages.

Firstly, there's the psychological advantage.

A few days day sailing will help the crew get to know each other, the yacht, and your style of leadership before being thrown into a long and, for novice yachtsmen, possibly a worrying passage. It will also help you get to know your crew, and identify any possible issues or weaknesses (such as undeclared sea sickness or inability to stand a watch without supervision).

For most people, sea sickness is overcome after a few days of getting used to the particular motion of the yacht, so an initial sail might well help to relieve any rough stomachs before the Biscay crossing.

There is, however, the converse risk that someone who is sea sick for the first few days, seeing a landfall approaching in Dartmouth or Falmouth, might be very tempted to get off. It can take a lot of persuasion to keep them on board until they've got their sea legs. But it's often worth doing, even if it means sailing a little further down the coast to Falmouth to achieve it. I suffer for the first few days of a passage if I've not been to sea for a while, but I know that after those few days, everything settles down and my stomach gets used to the motion. And then I start loving it!

Secondly, there's the command structure to consider.

If you are sailing with crew you've not sailed with before, although you may have their sailing CVs to give you some insight into their skills and experience, you won't want to make important decisions like appointing a first mate without seeing how the crew interact with each other.

And in the worst case, if you find there's someone who really can't take it and wants to get off (or you decide they need to leave the yacht), you're still in the UK and can manage it with the least inconvenience for everyone.

Thirdly, there's the physical advantage.

By making a day sail as your first leg, you'll be able to shake down the yacht on a relatively short passage, so that any faults can be identified and fixed whilst you're still in the UK. There's nothing worse (as Michael Perham discovered on his single-handed round the world attempt) than starting out, then discovering a whole series of faults with the yacht that need repair, and having to fly out parts, or negotiate repairs in different currencies.

Fourthly, there's the weather advantage.

A weather forecast becomes less and less certain as the days progress. You can probably rely fairly well on a three or four day forecast, but any longer and the level of uncertainty increases. So positioning your yacht for a departure that shortens the Biscay crossing, whilst keeping you close enough to home should you need to wait out weather for more than a few days makes sense.

By positioning your yacht in the South West of England or Northern France, you're able to look for a decent weather window, and if you have to wait any length of time, you'll be in a nice place to do it. Dartmouth, Falmouth, the Channel Islands or even Camaret, Brest, or one of the anchorages in the Rade de Brest would suit if you need to wait for suitable weather and want the shortest crossing.

Gosport to Falmouth or Northern France

Let's assume that your positioning passage will be series of day sails from

Gosport to Falmouth. That's a passage of approximately 180 nautical miles.

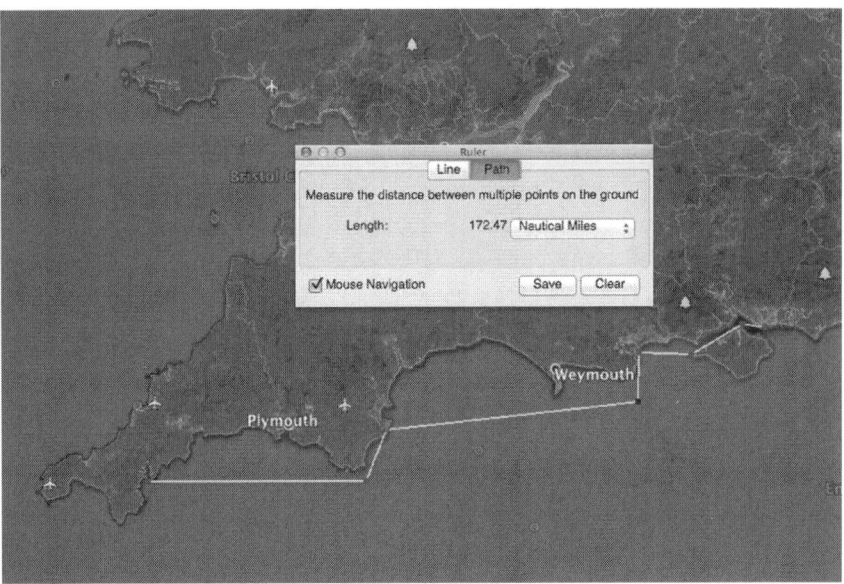

Google Earth helps you plan your first passage route.

This gives you quite a few options. Maybe a first day sail from Gosport to Poole, which will give you and your crew a gentle day sail to get to know each other, and will familiarise them with the yacht without pressure. The passage is only about forty nautical miles, which in a 45' yacht in fair weather should take you no more than six and a half hours at a planning speed of six knots.

An evening meal ashore, and then an early start for Dartmouth. That's a passage of around 75 nautical miles, which at a planning speed of six knots is likely to take you around twelve and a half hours. So, tides and wind permitting, an early start from Poole to get to Dartmouth in time for supper ashore. You'll need to work out how to negotiate the Portland race, though. Given that you're off to Dartmouth rather than Lyme Regis, there isn't much advantage in trying to sneak through the northern side of the race close in to the Bill, so you might as well head far enough south to miss it, and then turn west. Wind permitting, of course.

Dartmouth is a great stopping place, with very safe moorings up river. Beware of the partially submerged Mew Stone (well marked) if you're coming inshore from Brixham or Paignton though.

After a break in Dartmouth, it's on to Falmouth. This is a passage of about seventy nautical miles, and with the same planning speed it's going to take you just under twelve hours. Maybe a night passage to get the crew into the routine of night sailing, with perhaps a slight routing adjustment to pass close to the Eddystone lighthouse, which is always a high point for those who've not seen it before.

And an early morning arrival at Falmouth will give you and your crew a chance to rest, an arrival breakfast, a re-fuelling stop, and time either to prepare for the Biscay passage or, if you've planned the positioning passage a week or so before the long passage south to northern Spain, plenty of time to catch the train back home.

By positioning the yacht in Falmouth, not only will you have the option of some lovely west country sailing if you're staying any length of time, but you're also ready to get provisioned and prepared for the passage south.

Falmouth or Northern France to La Corunna

A departure from, say, Falmouth, and an arrival at La Corunna would be a passage of about 425 nautical miles. With a wind with a bit of north in it and reasonable weather it would take you just over three and a half days at five knots, or just over three at six knots. Tides permitting, you might plan to leave Falmouth very early in the morning to aim to get to La Corunna in time for an evening meal and a beer or two.

But there's another option. Falmouth to Camaret can be done in about a day. It knocks over one hundred miles off the Biscay passage, and gives you the chance to pick up some wonderful French bread, cheese and wine for the crossing. Not to mention a supper of Moules Mariniere. The crew might well welcome a stop in France, and being an EU country, there are no extra formalities to negotiate.

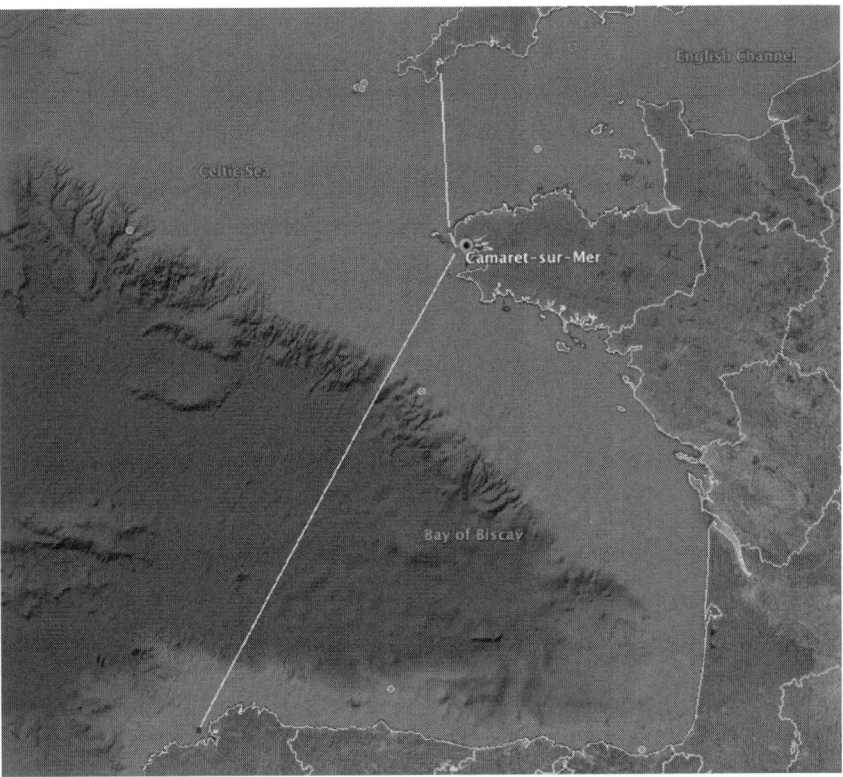

Falmouth to La Corunna via Camaret

Departing from Camaret, it's only 330 nautical miles to La Corunna, which will take you around two and a half days at an average six knots, and maybe even less with a fair wind. But you'd need to navigate the famous Chenal du Four, which, if you get fair weather and the tides right, can be great fun for all. Although it can be entered both in daylight and at night, it's best to navigate it in daylight, not only because of the large number of lights that all need to be identified if you're running the passage at night, but also because you'll be able to judge the smoothest water - it can get a bit more than choppy in North Westerlies, no matter what state of tide. So if you decide on this option, then you need to plan your departure from Falmouth to get you to the start of the Chenal at the best time. Read the pilot book!

Crossing Biscay

For many inexperienced yachtsmen, the idea of crossing Biscay is scary. It has a reputation, thoroughly deserved, for cutting up very rough in certain conditions. I've crossed it in a South Westerly force ten in a 45 foot yacht, and I wouldn't want to do that again in a hurry. The reason is in the contours of the sea bed. If you look at Google Earth again, you'll see that the deeper sea bed funnels into Biscay from the Atlantic in roughly a V shape. The sea bed rises dramatically from nearly six thousand feet to a few hundred at most. And with a strong westerly wind, huge quantities of water are pushed up against the rising continental shelf creating massive high, steep and confused seas.

But in good weather, Biscay can be calm with balmy, warm winds, dolphins, and wonderful starry nights. You just need to pick a good weather window before you depart. If you get the weather right, then Biscay can be a dream crossing.

And going direct really is the safest route. Inexperienced crew might wonder why you don't sail round the inside of the bay, staying close to land. But this is a dangerous option.

Firstly, departing from Camaret it will lengthen the passage from around 330 nautical miles to around 670, a little over twice the distance, increasing the time from under three days to over five and a half.

Secondly, south of the Gironde river there are really no ports of refuge at all until you get to Northern Spain.

Thirdly, just south of the Gironde is a huge French military restricted zone which you would have to avoid.

Fourthly, the water gets very shallow indeed as you travel towards San Sebastian and there are no ports of refuge, so if you get caught in bad weather you really are in trouble. The prevailing winds all have a good degree of westerly in them, so you're likely to be embayed. Steep short seas are nasty, but as the water gets shallow, those seas become breaking waves, and breaking waves are dangerous: they can easily roll a yacht. It's happened.

If Biscay really does worry you, then you can shorten the crossing by going from La Rochelle to Bilbao, a passage of only 190 nautical miles. But it won't help you get to Gibraltar any quicker, and you'll have all the problems of fog and strong winds along the north coast of Spain to worry about. However, the advantage of this route (possibly the only advantage) is that the north coast of Spain is a lovely sailing area, with steep eucalyptus covered mountains, interesting rias, and some wonderful food.

Unless you want to take in some of the north coast of Spain, by far the best approach is to pick your weather window and go straight across.

Landfall in Northern Spain

One of the things to beware when crossing Biscay is getting embayed. Some will tell you that concerns about being embayed belong to the square riggers of the past. Whilst that's partly true, it still applies today. With south westerly winds prevailing, it's too easy to get further into the bay as you head south, and then find that you are well and truly headed and can't easily round Finisterre, which must be done with a good offing. So with winds with any west in them (which is most of the time), it pays to head out into the Atlantic a bit before you head south, so that you have plenty of sea room to make La Corunna, if that's where you want to end up. Again, it depends on reading the winds effectively. You might be able to gain sufficient sea room to round Finisterre simply by sailing west from Land's End for a bit before heading South.

There are other good landfalls for the Biscay crossing, though. If you do find yourself on the inside of the bay, you can happily head for the Ria de Viveiro. It's an easy entrance, with a very sheltered, if small, marina in Viveiro. The pub on the water front does wonderful 'Pulpo', or fried Octopus. Or you can anchor in the bay in all but Northerlies, which cause quite a swell.

Alternatively, if you're well on the outside of the bay and can round Finisterre easily, then Vigo or Bayonne could be a better option than La Corunna. You'll be that much further south, and will have passed the worst of the Finisterre weather.

Stay flexible

Reading the wind is key, and being flexible in the way you approach a change of plan is equally important. It's no good bemoaning the fact that you've got yourself well and truly embayed; trying to fight both wind and weather round the corner of Finisterre is a risky option. A safe skipper will accept the change of circumstances, think through the implications of any change of plan on the passage and his crew, and then make plans for an alternative landfall. His next step will be to give a full briefing to his crew, so that they're not left wondering. There's nothing unfortunate about exploring one of the Rias of Northern Spain – the food in Galacia is wonderful, and too many Yachtsmen sail right past this interesting part of the coast.

As an aside, although it's a convenient and well known landfall and departure for a Biscay crossing, we've never yet failed to pick up some abandoned bit of fishing gear as we enter La Corunna. There's a big fishing port just north of the entrance, and I'm sure that a lot of fishermen dump their broken gear into the sea as they approach home. I've had everything from net around the prop to a bag full of footballs trailing from the rudder. And it's not just me – several colleagues have told me of similar problems along that part of the Spanish coast. So if you're planning on La Corunna, carry a mask, flippers and a sturdy knife, or be prepared to call out the diver once you're alongside.

Corunna to Gibraltar

The third leg, from La Corunna down to Gibraltar, is a passage of roughly 620 nautical miles, which, if you were sailing it non-stop at a planning speed of five knots, would take you just over five days, or just over four at six knots. But again, you're unlikely to want to rush it, and there are some great places to visit on the way. Lisbon is fun, though some of the marina entrances are not easy to spot. And there's always Cascais if you don't want to run up the river.

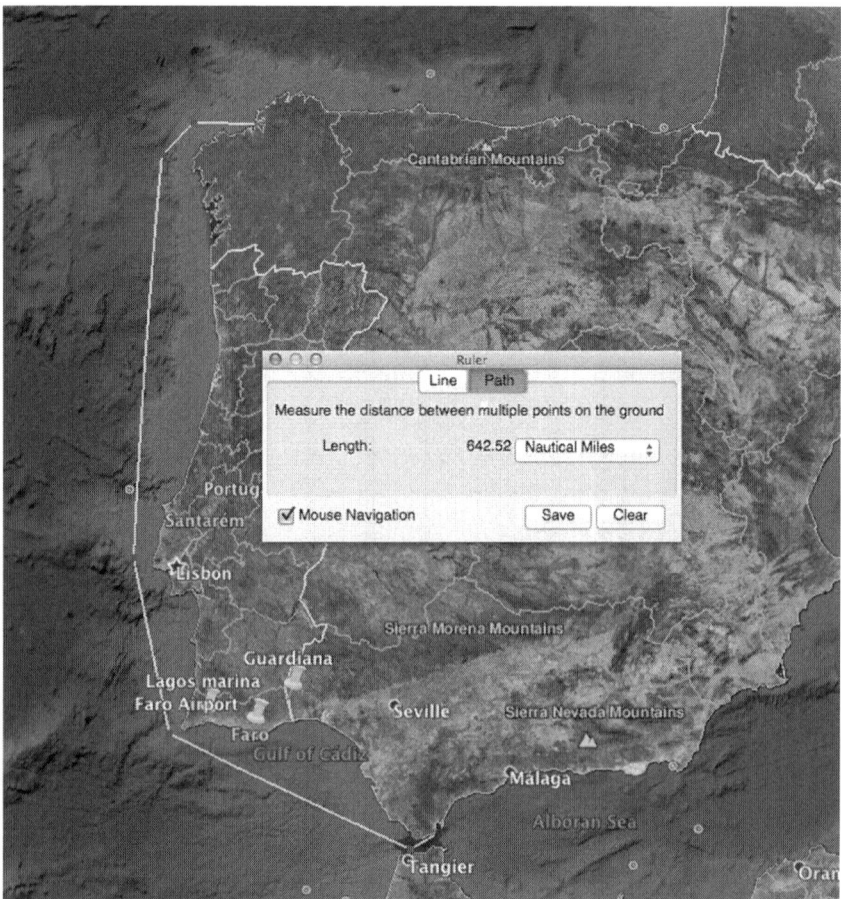

La Corunna to Gibraltar

Be careful as you head south from Vigo. The coast becomes flatter, the sea more shallow, and many of the ports on the Portuguese coast are unsafe in bad weather. There've been some very nasty accidents along that bit of coast when yachts have tried to enter a marina closed because of adverse winds. The Portuguese authorities don't close ports because they can't be bothered to keep them open, but because of the real danger of entering in shallow water and rough seas. Again, it pays to read the pilot book carefully and plan what you're going to do if the weather turns against you.

Once you turn into the strait as you head for Gibraltar, you'll find the conditions may well change. From the balmy warmth of the Atlantic coast of Portugal and southern Spain, you move to the peculiar conditions of the strait, where shipping, fog and adverse winds often upset the carefully made passage plan.

Again, it pays to read the pilot book carefully before entering the strait, but taking advantage of the easterly flowing current in the middle isn't always wise if there are adverse winds: these can kick up a strong wind over tide chop that can get nasty, and it will be a much slower passage. It's not for nothing that Tarifa is the surfing capital of Spain. Careful planning requires a good local weather forecast and an understanding of the tidal effects through the strait. Again, reading the pilot book will help.

Time constraints

Almost always, you're going to have a set of constraints within which to work. The first of these is usually time. Unless you and your crew are all retired or free of work commitments, you are often tied to holiday dates – at least for some of your crew if not for you. So let's presume that you are self-employed or retired and have the flexibility to take up to six weeks to do the passage. You're not sure at this stage about crew or availability, so the best thing to do is to make an outline plan, and then share your plans and see if you have the makings of a crew.

The first leg, the positioning and shakedown cruise, can be done over a long weekend if the weather is good, or a five day week if not. In five days, you'll almost certainly be able to get to Cameret or one of the marinas in north western France if that's your choice.

In fact, the choice of where to position may well be determined more by crew availability than passage preference.

Given reasonable weather, your passage from South West England or Northern France on down to Gibraltar can reasonably be done in a fortnight, which is ideal for people who are constrained by holiday dates.

And here's a tip: the British Airways flights from Gibraltar back to the UK are very much cheaper if you buy the ticket in Gibraltar. Check online if you want confirmation. I am guessing that there's some form of subsidy from the UK government, or at least some agreement with BA, because it's worked for me in the past. There's usually plenty of availability, and booking when you get to Gibraltar avoids that horrid pressure of worrying about missed flights if you're held up by weather or structural problems.

And if time really is against you, and either you or your crew can't get the necessary days off, there's always the option of a delivery crew. The cost may well be offset by the saving of time in having your yacht in Gibraltar or the Spanish Islands so that all you need to do is just 'step on board'.

Knowing the issues

As you study each bit of the passage, reading the pilot books and talking with other skippers, you'll soon form a good mental map of the issues you're going to face.

On the first leg, you've got the tidal gates at Hurst Castle (if you come through the Solent), the race off St. Alban's head, the much more serious Portland Race, and the tidal gate off Prawle Point.

On the Biscay leg you've got the initial decision about whether to run out west before turning south to avoid being embayed, a decision that depends both on wind direction and weather patterns. You've got the option of where to make landfall if embayed, or a better port if you get exceptionally good weather, are ahead of your planned time, and can leave Finisterre well to port. And most important of all, you've got to decide on the 'go / no go' criteria for departure, which will certainly have weather as the major factor, but may also include such things as crew fitness and any yacht issues you have discovered.

You will have more flexibility on the leg from northern Spain down to Gibraltar, but again, weather will play a key part in your decision-making. And you will be aware of the biggest risk of all – time pressure.

Never, ever, let the pressure of having to be somewhere by a certain date cause you to take unnecessary risks. Much better to leave the yacht in a port short of your destination in order to complete the passage later, in safer conditions, than to press on with a tired crew in marginal or unsafe conditions.

Final detailed planning

Once you have the outline of the passage in your head, you can start putting your waypoints into your navigation software. Even if you don't yet have access to the yacht's chart plotter, you can make a list, or use something like iSailor on your iPad for the detailed preparation work.

But you can only make your final passage plan decisions when you know your crew availability, so the next step will be to get the word out and recruit your crew.

STEP FOUR - KNOWING YOUR CREW

Recruiting and managing a crew is a lot more than issuing a few vague invitations, sorting out a watch system and giving instructions about the passage.

A good skipper thinks hard about which crew to invite and how the accommodation is going to work, gets to know them well enough to help them overcome any concerns or shortcomings, delegates specific tasks (in advance where possible) to make the most of their skills and experience, and helps them to get the very best from their time on board. A skipper is also responsible for crew discipline where necessary, and for someone who's not dealt with any form of personnel management this can be a daunting task.

But a skipper who's focused entirely on moving the yacht from A to B without any consideration of how the crew are feeling, what they have to offer, or what they might want from the passage, won't keep regular crew for long and might even lose a few during the passage itself.

As we will see later when we look at heavy weather sailing, one of the things that can help settle an anxious crew member is having a measure of control. Even if that control is limited to a specific job, it can be a great help. So delegating key tasks in advance isn't just for your own convenience (though it's a great help), but is also a good crew management tool for those who might be more than a little anxious about making a long passage with you.

Finding Crew

How you get crew will vary hugely from skipper to skipper. You may have a long list of people who you like to sail with, or a tighter and smaller group who make up your regular crew and who have already said they'd be willing to do a longer passage with you. You may be sailing with family members and their friends. Or you may have to advertise on something like Crew Seekers, or join one of the many crewing groups. The Cruising Association run a brilliant crewing scheme that puts skippers and potential crew in touch with each other.

Delegation

On even a short passage, you won't be able to do everything yourself. And neither should you try. One of the marks of a safe, competent skipper is that he or she appears to others to have little to do. The reality is different, of course. But with proper delegation, a reasonable understanding of the competence and experience of your crew, and a watchful eye on progress, you should be able to delegate a fair bit of the work and give yourself time to reflect, to watch, to make those small changes or give that bit of extra encouragement that makes all the difference to the way your crew see you.

A good skipper is a relaxed skipper. You'll often find a good skipper appearing simply to observe what's going on, maybe simply observing the passing coastline or the way the crew is working together. Externally he or she will appear to be doing very little, quietly enjoying the moment. In reality, he or she may well be going over the passage plan, considering watch changes, or even thinking about the next meal. But a good skipper is more often found on deck. Rarely will a good skipper spend his or her time running the yacht from the chart table.

If you sail regularly with someone you consider to be the first mate, especially if that's your life partner, then it pays to involve them in the decisions about who to invite as crew. You might even delegate the routine process of sending out invitations, drawing up joining instructions, organising trial sails, and so on, to your trusty first mate. The more you can delegate, the better. Your crew will know that you trust them, they'll have something concrete to concentrate on when things get difficult, and you will become the conductor of a finely tuned orchestra, rather than a one-man-band trying to bang a drum whilst playing a guitar and singing at the same time.

In fact, delegation is one of the hallmarks of a good skipper. I once skippered a week's charter around Mallorca. Not exactly testing, but one of the crew had been a submarine engineer. Very early on, I asked him if he would be willing and would enjoy being the yacht's engineer for the week. He was very happy to accept, and it meant that the daily engine checks were done well. When we had a problem with the holding tank later in the week, he was able to come up with a novel solution that only a submariner would have been able to carry through!

How you divide the responsibilities is up to you. The aim should always be the most comfortable and safe management of the yacht. But part of the business of crew selection for any long passage is matching the skills and experience of the crew to the needs of the passage.

But however you structure the crew management tree, you should always respect the 'chain of command' that you have set up.

The Chain of Command

Which brings me neatly to one of the key issues in crew management, which is respecting the chain of command. One of the most important skills that will make you a safe skipper is understanding the importance of the relationship between authority, command, and delegation, and the roles you are going to have to take to exercise them.

Authority, command and delegation

As skipper of a sailing yacht, you are in sole charge. This isn't a matter of agreement amongst the crew - you are not elected to the position. Nor is it a matter of inevitability if you are the owner – you don't have to be the skipper. But once you accept the position, it's a fact of law. The moment you assume command, you accept the responsibilities that go with it. And many of these have legal consequences. The technical word for your position on the vessel is Master, and as Master of the vessel under your command, you have absolute responsibility for the safety and well-being of your crew, the safe management and navigation of the yacht, and for ensuring that your actions and the actions of your crew don't endanger or inconvenience other vessels.

Age isn't a factor. It doesn't matter if you are relatively young. In the days of the old Clipper ships, the Masters were often in their early twenties. They were still known affectionately (or not so affectionately) as 'The Old Man', and they were highly respected for their skills and abilities. With the clipper races of the 19th Century, they were the pop stars of the day.

What matters is firstly your experience and skills in sailing the yacht. If you don't know what you're doing, then you're better off finding another skipper and learning from them before taking command. But if you have reasonable sailing skills, and know how to manage the yacht and the crew, you'll learn how to make the right kind of decisions. We all have to learn somewhere, and mistakes, particularly in the management of the crew, are good teachers. In Thai, there's a saying which, roughly transliterated, is Phit ben Kru. Mistakes are your teachers. You're going to make them. So learn from them.

Your First Mate is key

Even in a small yacht with a crew of three, you will be wise to designate a 'second in command' just in case something happens to you. Whenever I sail, and even if it's only with a small crew, I'll appoint someone to take command should anything happen to disable me, and I'll make sure the crew know. And when I practice a 'man overboard', I will sometimes say 'Skipper overboard' just to test the reaction of the crew to the alternative command structure.

The traditional term for a 'second in command' on a yacht is 'First Mate'. In a crew of three, the traditional structure would be 'Skipper' as Master, 'First Mate' as the second in command, and 'Third Mate' or 'Crew'.

With a crew of five, you might have the Skipper, and two watches consisting of a 'Watch Leader' and a 'Crew Member' each. Or with a crew of seven, you might have a Skipper and three watches of two. With eight on board, you might have both the Skipper and First Mate as 'floating' crew who don't keep watches, but who divide the responsibilities of running the yacht between them. And in every case, there should be someone who knows, and is known by the crew, to be in command if anything happens to the skipper. It's also good self-interest: if you go overboard, you want the command structure to operate quickly and automatically. You don't want the crew holding a conference to decide who does what!

With anything larger than a crew of three friends, respecting the chain of command is a vital part of welding a crew into a working unit. Your junior watch keepers will look to their watch leaders for direction, support and encouragement. Your watch leaders will look to the First Mate as their immediate superior. And your First Mate, if he or she is to maintain his or her authority, will not only look to you for leadership, but will need you to respect his or her own leadership position and not contradict it.

That means that in a large yacht, the management of the crew is likely to be run by through your first mate. Note 'through', not 'by'. If you're going to make changes to the watches, they are best discussed first with the First Mate, who will then pass on the decision to the watch leaders. If there's an issue you notice with a crew member, your best way of dealing with it is to ask the First Mate to raise it with their watch leader. Maintaining a good relationship with your First Mate is crucial to the running of a happy crew.

This 'chain of command' is as important on a small yacht as it is in a large ship. Imagine how you would feel if you were the First Mate, and the Captain kept giving instructions direct to the watch leaders? You might well begin to resent being left out. And you'd be right. One of the key ingredients in managing and keeping a happy yacht is making sure that you respect the various crew positions. They have worked hard to get their experience, they deserve your respect, and it's a basic human need to know where in the pecking order they stand.

If you are uncertain of your crew's strengths and weaknesses, especially if you've not sailed with them before, then there's no need to designate positions before they join. If there are two or more people who might have necessary experience to take on the position of first mate, there's no need to make any judgments until you've sailed with them for a few days.

I will always appoint someone to take over from me if I am incapacitated, but I make it fairly clear, without spelling it out, that this is a 'pro tem' arrangement. I can even nominate different first mates for each shake down leg on the basis that it's good to give different people experience of the position. When I've got a reasonable idea of the strengths and weaknesses of the crew, and of their personalities, I will then make a decision and take my first choice aside and ask him or her if he or she would be willing to take on the role of first mate for the passage. If they agree, then I'll discuss with them the remaining crew structure and will agree a watch structure.

This does mean that the larger the crew, the more distant you are likely to be from your junior watch keepers. One way of bridging that distance whilst keeping the chain of command intact is to use praise. If I notice something that a junior crew member has done that is particularly good, I will often take them aside, particularly if it's early in the passage, and show that it hasn't gone un-noticed. A quiet word of praise from the skipper can do wonders for crew morale and satisfaction. It often works with difficult crew members as well, where even the smallest good action can be recognised and acknowledged.

Making decisions

You may need to ponder, to think, to consider alternatives, to change your mind a few times. Do it, but do it privately. By all means consult the first mate as part of the process. But only when you have made your decision should you brief the crew accordingly. There's nothing more calculated to cause an inexperienced crew to lose confidence in the command than a continuing 'shall we, shan't we' approach. By all means, listen to any objections voiced at the briefing. Explain why you have dismissed that option, or if necessary, adjust to include it. But you need to maintain the authority of the chain of command. It's essential for a happy, well managed yacht.

Crew administration

If you know your potential crew members, it's a great advantage. But you may well have to make judgments about which crew to invite without having met them or sailed with them. A telephone conversation can help, but ultimately your own instincts will prevail.

I often tell my students that whilst I can teach almost anyone to sail, I can't teach someone who 'knows it all' to fit in with the other members of the crew. Attitude is a lot more important than skills. If I'm faced with a choice between someone whose paper qualifications look superb but who comes across as awkward or difficult in some way, and someone with lesser qualifications but who seems to be much more amenable, I'll choose the latter.

Whatever recruitment process you use, you will ultimately end up with a short-list of people to invite. The key thing with invitations is to be very honest about the passage and the yacht. It's about managing crew expectations. Most potential crew members are expecting to be challenged in some way, so a difficult passage or a less than ideal yacht may not put them off.

Whenever I recruit crew, I always send them (or ask the first mate to send them) a crew joining form which asks for things like full name, address, next of kin, passport number, issuing authority and expiry date, as well as personal information. I won't have smoking on my yachts (it's not just a personal aversion to smoke; there is real risk of damage to fiberglass and sails as well as the risk of fire) so being clear about that and about any other restrictions is an opportunity for potential crew to refuse the invitation. Choosing a long sea passage as a time to quit smoking, especially if it's not voluntary, isn't always sensible because it can result in fraught nerves all round!

Along with the joining form, I sometimes send out a standard set of basic 'standing orders' so that crew will see how I run the yacht. I have included, in Appendix 2, a copy of the basic standing orders that I use for all passages.

For a leisure orientated sail commanded by a very part-time skipper, these things might seem like over-kill. But my experience is that crew actually appreciate it because it sets out the boundaries very clearly, and demonstrates a professional and seamanlike approach to the passage even before it's begun. And if a potential crew member isn't going to like following safety rules, it's better to know about it before they join.

Sleeping Arrangements.

The sleeping arrangements will vary with each yacht, and it's vital that you think about them before you make a final decision on crewing.

I well remember one of my first trips as a young skipper. I'd chartered a 36' yacht for a long weekend on the Solent. I was in a fairly low paid job at the time, and for me the biggest worry was the cost of it all. Would I be able to fill the yacht? Would the crew be willing to pay? She was advertised by the charter company as an eight berth yacht - two double rear cabins, two single berths in the forepeak, and the saloon table would lower to create a double berth in the saloon. That's eight people. Having never done it before, I added up the cost of the charter, the estimated cost of food for three meals a day, added a bit for marina charges, then divided by eight. The final sum was reasonable, and I started my crew recruitment on that basis.

The crew ended up as all blokes, thankfully. Eight fairly large blokes. When I went on board and started allocating berths, I realised immediately that I'd made a huge mistake. I hadn't understood the yacht layout. Trying to put two large blokes and all their kit in each of the rear 'cabins', which were little more than two large coffins either side of the cockpit which could only be accessed horizontally, was going to be a nightmare for them. The forepeak was OK, provided the occupants were each less than five and a half feet tall. And the occupants of the double saloon berth were going to have to wait until everyone else was settled before lowering the table and sorting out the cushions.

There was one 'heads', and I failed to give what has become one of my standard briefings about not worrying about noise or waking people up if you need to use the heads in the night, nor did I mention the need to give at least twenty pumps on the flush.

I spent the first twenty four hours expecting my first mutiny. But thankfully, the crew were as new to sailing as I was to skippering, and although the result was huge embarrassment on my part, which I think I disguised fairly well with a show of 'its all lads together', the participants all seemed to assume that this is what sailing involved, and put up with it. But I won't forget the sight of two very large blokes in each of the coffins either side of the cockpit well!

We actually had a good weekend. It was very wet and our dry discipline was non-existent, resulting in a damp boat, a damp set of clothes, and general dampness all round. The food planning went reasonably, except that we consumed the entire weekend ration of breakfast on the first morning. But even that potential disaster didn't really matter, partly because one of the crew had a love of shopping and came back from the first trip ashore loaded with eggs, bacon, tomatoes and other sundries, and partly because I'd catered for all meals on board, but as soon as we moored up on the first night, the entire crew decided that they needed to get off the boat to discover the nearest pub that sold food as well as beer!

Don't overcrowd your yacht

The lessons learned on that trip were considerable. First of all, don't overcrowd your yacht. A small aft cabin might be suitable for a married couple, or at least a couple who don't mind being rather close to each other at night, but it isn't suitable for two large strangers unless there's sufficient room for privacy.

And the older your crew, the more privacy they need. Children seem to be able to bunk together in all sorts of crowded corners. But you shouldn't try putting two fifty five year old blokes together in one small after berth.

In fact, sleeping arrangements can continue to be a problem even for experienced delivery crew.

One of my more recent deliveries involved an Island Trader 40, a motor-sailor that had completed a single handed global circumnavigation. The layout had been modified for single handed operation. There was a huge double berth in the forward cabin, but the mattress was so far off the deck that falling off would have been a life-threatening event. It was absolutely no use for sleeping on at sea without modification. The cabin itself had been stripped of its U shaped seat and saloon table, leaving only the single berth to starboard.

It was an ideal arrangement for a single handed operation. You could sleep on the single berth in the saloon and keep an eye on the radar, windex and other instruments without leaving your berth. Fine for the skipper, but where were the two crew going to sleep?

I ended up fitting a kind of lee-cloth arrangement in the forward cabin, and divided the large double bed into two sea berths using a rope and a double sheet bought from a hotel supplier. The look on the faces of my crew when I confidently showed them how it would work was a picture, and we ended up with an inflatable bed on the cabin sole, and with one crew member sleeping on deck in harbour. It was a delivery, so we all expected to rough it a bit, but again, it was a lesson in crew management, which in this case meant allowing the crew to sort themselves out, with one sleeping in the cockpit well from time to time.

Catering

There's a huge difference between catering for a weekend day sailing and a long, watch-keeping passage of several days or more. The second lesson I learned was that when you're day sailing, you only really need to cater for breakfast (big and cooked) and lunch (bits and pieces, including cheese, bread and salad stuff). Provided you moor up somewhere near civilisation, the crew are usually glad to get off the yacht and find some restaurant or watering hole that provides food. So if you don't want to cater for dinner, moor up somewhere near a pub!

Don't forget the chocolate! Sailing is a very physical activity, and the requirement for calories goes up considerably when at sea. A tin or one of those plastic sealable containers full of small Mars Bars, Snickers, Ginger Biscuits (for those feeling a little 'queasy'), and other easily eaten treats is not only a very important morale booster, but can keep energy levels up. Forget the diet for a few days! Bananas are great for snacking if you're feeling a little sea sick, but they don't last too long. And eggs are brilliant as a comprehensive food. Scrambled, boiled, fried, or just mixed in with the spaghetti to make a Carbonara, eggs do it every time. Buy plenty of eggs! If you want them to stay fresh on a long passage, rub the shells with cooking oil - just enough to make them shiny and seal up the pores.

Catering is one of those activities that you will never get 100% right. It pays to ask each member of the crew to bring their favourite food, or at least to suggest additions to the shopping list, but only on the basis that they are prepared to share. Conflicts can very quickly arise if a crew member considers a particular food or drink to belong exclusively to them, and in order to avoid this, I make sure that all crew know that anything brought on board is available for all crew members, not just for themselves. Clearly, this doesn't apply to special foods needed for medical or health purposes, but these should be clearly marked and kept separate from the ship's stores.

Once it becomes known that Joe Bloggs particularly likes rolled oats for breakfast, and that he's provided the supply himself, other members of the crew tend to be considerate and allow him his fair share, so you can rely on basic human kindness to take care of the detail. And if you find that there's a crew member who steps out of line, a quiet word from their watch leader can often sort things out without you becoming directly involved.

Dealing with pests

I was on a yacht once where the owner had packed some Bisto gravy granules in one of the cupboards on a previous voyage. For those who don't know this wonderful British apology for gravy, it comes in granules largely made up of beef stock and corn flour. It's packed in a round cardboard container. But this particular container was peppered with neat, tiny round holes. It had become a nursery for bugs. The bugs turned out to be Cockroaches. The yacht was infested.

Getting rid of Cockroaches on board is entirely possible. Forget poisons; they don't work (cockroaches are immune to most of them), and they're a risk.

All you need is either a mixture of condensed milk and boric acid powder, or some diatomaceous earth, plus some hard work and some patience. The boric acid mixed with sweetened condensed milk can be left as cockroach bait, or the diatomaceous earth dusted onto shelves. Either will kill them over a period of a few days (it will kill ants, too). Dealing with the critters you can see is also fairly easy, as they come out at night. If you have a handy sprayer, fill it with water and washing up liquid. Even though roaches run fast, a few squirts with soapy water will disable and drown them, as the soap lowers the surface tension of the water sufficiently to prevent them breathing. A campaign like this, waged over a few days, coupled with improved food storage and hygiene, will work just fine.

Storing food so it won't attract pests

But if your food storage and garbage hygiene is up to scratch, you won't need to get rid of the pests.

Storing food on board a yacht is an art in itself. If you don't get the storage of your foodstuff right, you'll lose it. Or worse, you'll attract unwanted visitors. Sharing a yacht with cockroaches isn't enjoyable, and you really don't want to offer them an open invitation to dine with you. And you don't want to offer an open invitation to mice or other rodents. So don't leave it to an inexperienced crew member to stow the shopping without giving them a short lesson first. Here's a few tips, mostly learned the hard way, to help you avoid some of the nasties.

The aim of all food storage on board is (a) to keep it as fresh as possible thereby maximising its useful life, (b) to store it so that you know what you've got and what you've used, (c) to store it securely when it's not needed, and (d) to prevent it being consumed by unwanted guests.

The first rule is to remove all cardboard from your shopping and dump it ashore, storing the contents in sealed airtight plastic containers. All loose dry food should be stored this way. Cardboard food containers should be banned on board. As a medium for keeping cereals or other foods fresh, it's useless in a boat. If there's any raised humidity, it's one of the first things to go damp and soggy. But worse, the cardboard itself is a food that's loved by critters, and is also a nesting material for rodents and other pests. Bugs can easily bore their way through cardboard to get at the contents if they want.

Tins are fine, but they have paper labels which can quickly degrade in the damp so after a few weeks you won't know what's in the tins, particularly if you store them anywhere near the bilges or where condensation can form. Don't store them in cardboard boxes (no cardboard on board!). Use an indelible marker to write the contents on the lids, remove the paper labels, lightly wipe them over with an oily cloth to prevent them rusting, and store them so that you can read the tin lids. Make sure the marker really is indelible though, or you'll be playing a game of 'food roulette' later in the voyage.

You can keep eggs fresh for longer by wiping them with a thin layer of cooking oil to seal the pores. Fruit and veg last longer if (a) they haven't been refrigerated en route to the market, and (b) they are stored where the air can circulate. Eat the bananas first, and store onions away from potatoes. Examine the veg regularly, and eat any that is showing signs of degrading.

Rodents

Mice and Rats are very fond of yachting, and are a prevalent pest in most ports and marinas. But like humans, they need a way to get on board. The best way to stop them is to make sure that there isn't an unbroken path from the dockside to the yacht. Try to moor so that the yacht isn't hard against the dockside. If you use a passarelle, lift it so that it's a few inches above the dockside, and stow it when not in use. Gang planks should be stowed when not in use, particularly at night. All lines to the shore, including fender lines, should have rat catchers fitted. These can be as simple as a used plastic water bottle with the base cut off and the line threaded through the top. Rodents either fall off the plastic, or go up the inside of the bottle and get stuck.

Water

Water is an essential safety issue. Even if I know the yacht well, and trust the fresh water tank, I will always flush it a couple of times before setting out on any passage. Most skippers and owners have their own favourite ways of keeping the fresh water system fresh, and there are a number of different additives you can use to combat possible water bourn infections and contaminations.

Even a clean water tank will produce bad water if the lines are not clean. A shock treatment using eight ounces of household bleach for every ten gallons of water, run through the pipes (don't forget the wash basin in the forward heads) and then left for no longer than 24 hours before flushing twice with fresh water will get rid of most nasties. It's then a case of keeping the water fresh by using it.

But whatever method you use, you should also carry bottled water. A leak in one of the water pipes can dump your entire water supply into the bilge in very short order, and if you're at sea, there isn't any way of putting it back.

A good rule is one and a half litres per day per person with at least 25% spare. So a passage of five days with six people on board will see you loading and storing 57 litres of bottled water. It may seem like over-kill, but if you are becalmed and your water tank springs a leak, you're going to need it. And in the unlikely case that you need to take to the life raft, having plenty of bottled water with you is going to be reassuring to everyone.

One key thing to check before leaving harbour is how your fresh water supply is accessed. A fresh water supply that is only accessed by an electrical pump is going to be no use to you if the electrics fail. Some kind of manual pump is a good idea, but if you're stuck with only an electrical pump, check to see how else you might lift water from the tank. Can you syphon into a sterile container? Can you tap from the water feed pipe in the bilge? If the answer is 'no', then a spare supply of bottled water is essential.

A 'no blame' culture

I have a rule on any yacht that I skipper. It's that we try, as far as possible, to operate a 'no blame' culture. I want everyone from my first mate to my junior deck hand to raise a question about the management or navigation of the yacht if he or she thinks there's a danger or risk to safety. Whilst you don't want to foster a culture where every decision is questioned and second guessed by your junior watch keepers, you don't want to be so far removed from your crew that they don't bring a dangerous issue to your attention. And if something happens, you want to learn from it. Fear of being 'found out' and consequently blamed can lead to the failure to report potentially dangerous issues.

In many Accident Investigation Board reports, failure by the first officer to challenge a captain's decision when the first officer is aware of a risk or a dangerous mistake is one of the contributing factors in too many accidents. In my initial safety briefing, I outline the need for developing this culture, and although it can sometimes be difficult to maintain when someone repeatedly makes stupid mistakes, it's worth trying hard to foster it.

Making it Fun

One of the key skills of a good skipper running a volunteer crew is recognising that your crew members are in it for fun. They want to enjoy their sailing. And knowing what each of them enjoy about sailing will help. So part of your job will be to try to make sure that it's fun for your crew. And each of them will have different ideas about what they want.

Fairly early on in any passage, I try to spend a short time with each crew member to ask them if there's anything in particular that they'd like to get from the passage. It might be brushing up on their navigation skills, learning how to use the radar, or even how to stream a fishing line. You could be surprised by what comes from such a short conversation.

And then, if you possibly can, try to fit it into the passage planning. It can make all the difference, and can win people to you particularly if you don't know them all that well.

And if there's a choice of port along the way, and it makes little or no difference to your passage plan, it can be a good idea to sound out the crew. Not only will it give at least some of the crew a chance to visit a place they'd like to see, but it may also deflect any possible criticism from you about the choice of harbour. After all, if they've chosen to go there, they're not going to blame you too much if it doesn't live up to expectations.

Encourage your crew

Encouragement is very important. Don't overdo it, but if you see a junior member of the crew do something particularly well, or take a bit of initiative in preventing an incident, then do have a quiet word with them to praise them. I will never forget one of my early skippers who did just this with me. I was a nervous, uncertain deck hand and one day spotted a lashing that had come undone on the liferaft. I pointed it out to the watch leader, who repaired it. But the skipper had noticed, and quietly took me aside and told me that I had done well to spot it and had taken the right action. It did wonders for my confidence, as well as my respect for that skipper.

Dealing with problems

Hopefully, the only problems you are going to face with your crew will be the occasional bout of sea sickness coupled with an initial nervousness on first leaving the harbour. But there are other potential difficulties, especially if you're sailing with people you don't know.

One of the questions you need to settle fairly early on is who, precisely, is going to be responsible for crew discipline and how the process will work.

Of course, ultimately, it will be you. But if you're running a larger yacht with six or eight crew and have a first mate, it can be helpful to agree with your first mate how discipline issues, if any, are to be dealt with. You might talk over your key areas of concern in general terms, such as being fit to sail after a party ashore, or smoking, or being late on watch, or not doing the cooking or washing up - whatever the issues are - and agree a process before the need to implement it.

This can also help to reinforce the chain of command that's so important.

Sea Sickness

There's a whole raft of advice about dealing with sea sickness, and all of it is relevant because in my experience, there isn't a single 'cause and effect'. Often, it's a combination of fear and motion, coupled with being cold. Provided the victim isn't too far out of it, you can help with all three.

First of all, and most important, I stress the huge importance of keeping warm. Never, ever, under any circumstance, allow yourself to get cold. It's advice that's given to RNLI crew members because it's good advice. Hammer it home, particularly with those crew members who might be likely to get sea sick. I've been there. Feeling a bit queasy, the energy levels drop and the thought of going below to change into something warmer isn't attractive. Sitting there with inadequate clothing, getting progressively colder, is a recipe for illness. It takes forever to warm up again. And at sea, hypothermia is a constant concern.

Dealing with sea sickness is important. First of all, you need to explain the problem clearly. I can do so with authority, because I suffer if I haven't been to sea for a while. But after a few days, my body adjusts to the motion and the environment, and I find myself enjoying life again. And this is what I explain to those who start to suffer. If they can be convinced that they can adjust, then it's half the battle won.

Giving the victim something to do will help with the fear aspect. Put them on the helm. That way, not only will they have to concentrate on steering a course, which takes their mind off the problem, but they will also have to look at the horizon, which helps their brain to adjust to the motion. Make sure they are warm, though.

One of the real problems of sea sickness is lethargy, and this combined with not wanting to go below to put on warmer clothing can quickly lead to a lowering of their core temperature that can be dangerous. If you do suspect that they are too cold, then insist on them putting on something warm. Give them a warm drink, and if necessary, put them in their bunk in their sleeping bag to warm up. It's helpful to delegate someone to keep checking on them, not just to make sure they're safe, but to keep them engaged with the passage.

If they do have to miss a watch, try to get them up for the next one so that the routine isn't too badly broken.

Sometimes, the initial bout of sea sickness can last a couple of days and gradually get better, but provided there's plenty of fluid taken in, recovery is often accompanied by a huge appetite! However, if it doesn't get better, you may have to consider putting the victim ashore.

Putting someone ashore because of an initial bout of sea sickness from which he or she can recover is always a mistake. It confirms in the mind of the victim that they're not really able to spend time at sea, when the reality may be very different. And that's not good skippering.

So it's worth trying to get the victim to work through it. One way of doing this is to have an end date in mind - say, three days - and to plan to visit a particular marina in that time. You can say to the victim that if they're not recovered by then, they have the option of cutting short the passage. And then work on them. Get them up to helm, or get them pulling lines, or even working as a lookout. It's surprising how often someone recovers in that time, and then stays on to enjoy the rest of the voyage. But if they're not much better after three days, it's a probable that they won't enjoy the passage and that they're not going to be much help as crew.

Alcohol

Most of us like to let our hair down occasionally, and going ashore for the first few times is an ideal opportunity. But putting to sea with a hangover isn't much fun. If there's going to be a big party ashore before leaving, then a short passage to an anchorage and a day's 'preparation' to get over the excesses can work wonders. That way crew can sleep it off, get used to the motion of the yacht, and keep clear of temptation!

But it's not easy to deal with more persistent offenders unless you're willing to have a 'dry' yacht. If you do have a problem with a crew member who can't regulate their alcohol intake, then a quiet word in private can often help. Young crew members sometimes have to be taught how to behave around alcohol, and some seem to think that unless you're half cut all the time you're not a real sailor. It's up to you how you deal with this problem, but I tend to nurse the first serious occasion, warn on the second, final warning on the third, and put ashore on the fourth.

Again, having a crew agreement that includes the requirement to be fit and ready to sail when required can help because you can refer to it with the crew member concerned. I have on occasions sailed with chronic alcoholics who were quite capable of doing their job, but it's a bit of an issue in case they get seriously ill or started some kind of withdrawal. Again, my way of dealing with this issue is to have in place a crew agreement that sets out quite clearly what your policy is.

Smoking

Quite straightforward, this one. I operate a no smoking policy, no ifs, no butts. It's not just because, being a non smoker myself, I can't stand the smell of cigarette, pipe or cigar smoke. It's also because of the risk to the yacht. Even if you discount the risk of fire, there's always the possibility of a burning cigarette doing serious damage to the gel coat and leaving ugly marks just where people are going to sit or work.

What is not acceptable is not being clear about your smoking policy before a crew member signs up. Having a crew agreement and stating your smoking policy very clearly on it avoids all the unnecessary pain of discovery once aboard.

I have had crew members who have signed up knowing my policy, but who think they can have a sneaky cigarette 'off the stern' during a quiet night watch. They get the usual two warnings then ashore, and it's something I'm very strict about. But again, it's up to you. You're the skipper, and you might smoke like a chimney yourself!

Drugs

This is a definite 'no'. If the yacht is discovered to have illegal material of any sort on board, it can mean arrest for you as skipper and the impounding of the yacht. In some countries it can mean the death penalty. So seriously do I take this that I include in my crew agreement the following paragraph:

You will not bring on board any drugs, weapons, publications or other material proscribed by UK, EU, and other relevant jurisdictions. If your skipper has any concerns about this, you may be asked to submit your belongings and person to search or inspection. If you are found to be, or suspected of being, in breach of these terms it may result in your immediate dismissal from the vessel.

In the very rare case that you might need to carry out an inspection, there needs to be a formal process for this. The first mate, or some other crew member, needs to be briefed in advance to act as witness. The process then needs to be explained to the crew member in detail with the witness present. The crew member is then given the opportunity to present any illegal substance to you in front of the witness for disposal. If a search is necessary, and it discovers anything illegal, or even suspicious, then the crew member has to be put ashore. Then the whole process needs to be written up in detail in the log book, and signed by yourself and the witness. There isn't any leeway in this, because your own neck is on the line along with other crew members, as well as the yacht itself.

Other wayward behaviour

If it's not illegal, then it's manageable. And if it means going to the local police to get the guy (or girl) out of trouble, then it's up to you to do your best. A fine paid to the local authority is often better than a lost crew member.

And it's not always the young lad who gets into trouble. I once sailed with a family where the mum was clearly 'in charge'. We were at a Greek port of entry, and she had tied up in the ferry basin. I advised her to move, but as the owner, she wasn't going to budge. She duly went ashore with the yacht's papers, and was told in very short order by the port police to move herself and her yacht. An argument ensued and she came storming back to the yacht, clearly angry beyond words at her treatment.

I had to warn her that she was facing arrest if she didn't comply, and that not every country followed due process. She only calmed down when a few thousand tons of ferry began backing towards her yacht. It's amazing how fast you can move a yacht when you have to.

As skipper, it's up to you how you deal with the huge range of human behavior that will get presented to you by crew members. If possible, having a first mate to discuss things with, and who can act as a first point of discipline, keeping you in reserve for serious issues or final decisions, is a great way of managing things. But when the crew is small, it's going to be up to you. If it can't be blind-eyed, then you have to deal with it. Waiting around hoping it will go away will often only make things worse.

STEP FIVE - KNOWING YOUR SAILING SKILLS

There's never a time when you'll know it all, and if you're a good skipper, you'll never stop learning. But there's a basic level of sailing skills needed in order to be a good skipper.

These are the most fundamental set of skills for getting the very best out of the yacht, the wind and the sea. They embrace the basics of sail trimming, making the best use of wind and tide, and helming to run the yacht at her maximum efficiency.

Anyone can sail a yacht. But only a good yachtsman can sail a yacht well. And in my experience, sailing a yacht well begins with understanding the dynamics of sail trim.

It starts with sail trim

Sail trim can be a bit of a mystery to the inexperienced sailor. Most of us know the basics - letting out the main and the headsail as we come off the wind, or tightening the sheets as we come closer to the wind. But the rest can seem a bit like magic. Just a few simple steps will help you get the best from your sails no matter where the wind is coming from.

Trimming your sails to get the very best from your yacht will help you gain a knot or two, and so save an hour or two on a longer passage. But above all, it will ease the load on your crew, and the helmsman will love you for it.

The most important thing to remember is that the sail isn't a big sheet that the wind pushes along. A properly trimmed sail operates in two ways. The first is a simple 'resolution of forces'. In anything but a run, the wind will exert a sideways force on the yacht, and the keel will resist that sideways force. The result is a kind of 'squeezing' action that helps to push the yacht forwards.

But that's only part of the process.

The other part is that the sail shape operates on a similar principle to the wing of an aircraft, cutting the air in the direction of the airflow, pulling the yacht forwards in the same way a wing pulls the aircraft upwards.

As an aircraft flies through the air, the curve at the front of the wing, or its aerofoil shape, cuts the air creating a low pressure area on the top surface of the wing, and a high pressure area on the bottom of the wing. So the wing is both 'pulled' upwards by the low pressure above it, and 'pushed' upwards by the high pressure below it, lifting the whole contraption into the air.

If you've got them set correctly, the sails will have a similar gentle aerofoil shape, and the air flowing smoothly across them will create a high pressure area on the windward side, and a low pressure area on the leeward side. The keel will resist the sideways force and stop the yacht from going sideways, resolving the forces into a heeling moment and the forwards movement you want. The combination of 'squeezing' and 'lifting' produces the forward motion that hopefully gets us to the pub before closing time.

The trick to good sail trim is to shape the sail so that you get three things:

- maximum lift
- minimum heeling moment
- maximum forward movement

In order to achieve this, you need first of all to create as near a perfect aerofoil shape to each of the sails as you can, and then present it at the right angle to the wind.

To get the right shape, you need to manage two things: camber, and twist. The maximum camber, or the curve that gives the sail its aerofoil shape, should be about 35% to 40% aft from the luff, or cutting edge of the sail, and is adjusted mainly by the tension in the halyard.

The tighter the halyard, the further forward the point of maximum camber. On a decently cut suit of sails, it is possible to adjust the point of maximum camber by looking up at the seams of each sail, and putting tension on the halyard, or easing it off.

Twist is a bit more complicated, but ignore it and you'll never get the best from your sails. If you are sailing forward at, say, six knots, with a 20 knot wind on the beam, you will experience two wind forces.

The first is the 'true' wind blowing at 20 knots at right angles to your direction. The second is the wind your forward motion is creating, and it comes from dead ahead - in this case, all six knots of it.

The combination of the two creates the 'apparent' wind, which is what your sail actually experiences. Apparent wind is a combination of the true and the manufactured wind, and it always blows from further forward than the true wind if you are moving.

Because of surface friction with the sea, the apparent wind at deck level is usually a point or two further forward than the wind at the top of the sail. So if you don't put the correct twist into the sail, part of the sail could be stalled.

A headsail will naturally want to twist, and all you have to do is control the amount by the angle that the foresheet makes with the clew. On the headsail, this is managed by the position of the car, which usually runs on some form of traveller. On the mainsail, it's managed by the mainsheet or the kicker.

Presenting the aerofoil at the right angle to the wind is a matter of using the headsail sheet, the mainsheet, and the mainsheet traveller in the right way. Think of an aircraft wing: if the pilot tries to climb too steeply, the wing will stall. Equally, if you sheet in the sail too tightly, you'll stall the sail. You can back wind it too, by doing the opposite.

The final basic principle of sail trim is how full, or how flat, your sails are. When an aircraft slows down, the pilot will deploy flaps and slats to increase the camber of the wing. This gives him more lift, but also greater drag. When he's going faster, he reduces flaps and slats, effectively flattening the camber of the wing.

In a similar way, when the wind is light we want the sails to be fuller in order to create more lift; when it's blowing hard, we want the sails to be flatter so as not to overpower the yacht. And that's all done by managing the sheets and the outhaul. On the foresail, you tighten up on the foresheet, maybe moving the car back a bit to reduce the twist at the same time. On the mainsail, you can manage the fullness of the sail by using a combination of the out-haul, the mainsheet and the position of the mainsheet traveller.

So to recap the basic principles: to get the best shape to the sail, you will need to adjust the camber so that it's about 35% to 40% aft of the cutting edge, or luff, of the sail. You'll need to put in the correct amount of twist to allow for changes in the direction of the apparent wind at different heights, and you'll need to adjust the fullness of the sail to match the force of the wind. Think of it as the CTF of sail trim: Camber, Twist and Fullness.

Sail trim is an art and a science, and there's plenty written about it in much greater detail than I can cover here. If it's something that interests you, then read up about it, or go sailing with someone who can do it well.

Getting into the Groove!

It's one thing to set the sails more or less correctly, but there's a little bit more adjustment to do. It's called finding the 'groove'.

There's two ways of doing it: you are either sailing to the wind or sailing to the course. When sailing to the wind, you set an approximate course, set up the sails, then tweak your course until the yacht is sailing at maximum efficiency. Doing it the other way around is harder, because it's harder to feel when you've adjusted the sails correctly. As its easier to sail to the wind, let's work through that process.

First of all, choose a course into the wind that is as near to your intended course as possible, and get the helmsman to hold that course. Then start trimming with the foresail. Slacken the sail off until the leech is flapping and the sail is slack. Then move the traveller to about its mid position. Gradually tighten the foresheet until the leech stops flapping and then check the tell-tales. If the sail is flying with sufficient twist all the tell tales will be horizontal. More or less.

Then adjust the main. Depending on wind strength, adjust the outhaul either to flatten or fill the sail. Centre the traveller, tighten up on the kicking strap (but not too much if the sail needs to be full) and ease the mainsheet out. Watch the tell tales and the shape of the sail, and feel for the pull through your feet. When the sail is adjusted to approximately the right position, set the mainsheet at that point.

Now comes the interesting bit. Get the helmsman to harden up into the wind a little until the speed drops off, but not enough to cause the sails to backwind. Now, very very slowly, get the helmsman to ease away from the wind. Do this very slowly. You're feeling for the sweet point at which the yacht starts to heel, picks up speed, and starts sailing faster. On some yachts, it's very pronounced. On others, you have to repeat the exercise a few times to get the feel of it.

But once you're in the 'groove', tell the helmsman to steer to the wind, rather than the compass. He should always be feeling for that sweet spot. If he hardens up too much, then he needs to bear away until the sweet spot returns. If he bears away too much, the heel will increase and the speed will drop. One way of doing it is to try to keep the same angle of heel (difficult if the wind is a bit fluky), and it's a case of constantly 'feeling' for that point of maximum efficiency.

A hooked leech.

There are a couple of things to look out for. The first is making sure that the wind can flow off the back of the sail nice and sweetly. There is bound to be a bit of turbulence as the air flow on both sides of the sail meet up, but as far as possible, the flow off the back of the sail, the leech, should be soft and clean. However, there is usually a tensioning line that runs from the top to the bottom of the leech. If this is too slack, the leech will tend to flap about in the turbulence as the air comes off the sail. But if it's too tight, then the leech will tend to curl inwards, causing what's known as a 'hooked leech'.

A hooked leech is an 'orrible sight. Dreadful. It will spoil the shape of the sail and make trimming almost impossible. Unfortunately, some sails get damaged to the point where a hooked leech can't be unhooked. If that's happened to your sail, then it's time to visit the sail maker for repairs and adjustments. But usually a hooked leech can be unhooked by careful adjustment of the leech line.

Sometimes a headsail can have a tendency to inherent leech return, where the headsail turns inwards towards the mainsail. This isn't something you want, because it acts rather like the flaps on an aircraft wing, producing lots of drag, but in this case little lift, because the result is often back winding the main. One solution is to connect a second sheet to the clew and lead it outside the stay so that you are literally pulling the clew outboard, widening the gap. It's a trick used by many racing yachts, but it can be a bit of a pain to set up.

The exception is in very light airs, when a small amount of leech return is useful because it helps keep the foresail drawing, and gives sufficient 'feel' for the helmsman.

Parallel lines and a tight slot

As far as possible in anything other than very light airs, the leech of the foresail should be parallel with the luff of the mainsail, and at a maximum of seven or so degrees out from the centreline. That way, the air flowing through the slot between the two sails will be slowed sufficiently to create a strong differential between the inner and outer airspeeds, which results in increased drive for the yacht. Adjusting the width of the slot will have a beneficial effect on speed, but only if it doesn't result in a hook in the belly of the leech, which will slow the yacht and possibly even backwind the main.

Sailing with too much heel

We've all seen the pictures of racing yachts heeled right over with leeward decks awash. It makes for a great photo opportunity. But it doesn't make for efficient sailing. The reasons are fairly obvious when you think about them.

The further you heel the yacht, the less depth you have on the keel. This immediately produces three results. Firstly, you considerably increase leeway because there is less keel depth to stop the sideways moment of the yacht. Secondly, because more of the wind's force is being used to drive the yacht sideways, less of that force is being converted into forward movement. Thirdly, because of the increased leeway and the increased heel, more rudder is needed to maintain a course, increasing drag. The ultimate penalty will be a broach, but it's horrible to watch a helmsman struggling to keep a yacht from broaching just because she's over-canvassed and heeling like a one-legged rugby player.

Even a very slight easing of the mainsheet can result in a considerable reduction in heel. A few degrees of heel is both inevitable and welcome because it produces a slight weather helm for the helmsman to steer against, and helps balance the longitudinal forces between the headsail and the mainsail. But you really only need a few degrees of heel. Once you're in the groove, you can find that 'sweet spot' where the yacht picks up her skirts and runs by playing with the mainsheet and kicker, testing the yacht for different heel angles, and getting just the right amount of weather helm on the wheel or the tiller.

Rarely is it more than ten or fifteen degrees, which is probably good news for the duty cook and the off-watch sleepers.

If you can't get the yacht to sail without excessive heel, then it's time to reduce sail. Simple as that.

Weather helm and lee helm

Where the yacht wants to pull the yacht up into the wind, it's called 'weather helm'. Where it wants to push away from the wind, it's called 'lee helm'.

A yacht with both foresail and mainsail set and on a broad reach will have a pivot point. The wind force acting on the sail aft of the pivot point will tend to pivot the yacht towards the wind, creating weather helm. The wind force acting on the sail forward of the pivot point will tend to push the yacht away from the wind, creating lee helm. Getting the right helm balance is a matter of balance. No one really wants lee helm, so the final act of trimming the sails is a matter of balancing those two opposing forces so that you have just the right amount of weather helm.

A novice skipper might think that in the best of all possible worlds, when the foresail and the mainsail are properly balanced, the sails should steer the yacht with the rudder simply guiding her on her way. But very rarely will a yacht sail without the wheel or the tiller pulling the yacht either into the wind or away from it. And even if it does, it's not the most ideal sail trim.

A small amount of weather helm, say between two and five degrees, will actually help you to sail faster. This is because with weather helm, the rudder points slightly into the direction of the wind and works with the keel to generate lift in a similar way to an aircraft wing, and that will give you a very sight speed advantage.

It's also a safety feature. If you have a very slight weather helm and let go of the wheel or the tiller, the yacht will turn up into the wind and come to a standstill (or near enough). It's a bit like the pull-cord on an outboard motor - pull it and the engine stops.

And finally, having a little bit of weather helm on the tiller or the wheel gives the helmsman something to 'lean against'; it gives him or her much better feedback about how the yacht is behaving through the water.

Balancing the sails

So how do you change the balance to get the desired amount of weather helm?

In theory, there are two ways. You can either try to move the pivot point, or Centre of Lateral Resistance (CR), forward or aft, or you can change the amount of force on the mainsail or the headsail.

Balance is a dynamic, moving thing. It changes with wind strength, wind direction, angle of heel, sail trim and shape, and even with the distribution of weight fore and aft on the yacht.

So moving the pivot point forward or aft isn't as difficult as it might sound, and it can happen when you least want it. This can be very noticeable indeed on a modern beamy yacht, because as heel increases, far more of the hull is presented to the water on the leeward side, considerably increasing hull resistance on that side. At the same time, less of the hull is presented to the water on the windward side. This has the effect of pushing the pivot point forward with the result that the yacht turns to windward, sometimes very dramatically. So on a yacht with a very full beam, moving the crew to windward and trying to reduce heel will reduce weather helm and possibly avoid a nasty broach.

But on a large yacht, the weight of the crew sitting outboard isn't going to make that much difference. What's needed is a change in the sail plan.

The trim and set of your sails will determine whether the turning force, or 'Centre of Effort', is behind or in front of the pivot point, or CLR. If there's too much weather helm, you can try to move the CE forward a bit. You can do this either by reducing the force of the mainsail by easing the mainsheet, flattening the sail, or even by reefing it if you're near the point of over-canvassing the yacht. Or you can increase the draw on the foresail, perhaps by letting it fill a bit more, or by increasing the foresail area if you've got roller reefing and not all of the foresail is out.

Bearing in mind that more heel will increase weather helm, it pays to try to reduce sail area for balance rather than increase it, so reducing the draw on the main should help.

In the same way, if you're having problems with lee helm (which is much rarer in my experience), then increase the draw on the mainsail and reduce the draw on the foresail.

A more permanent solution

It is possible that no matter how much you play with the sails, your yacht still has a tendency for too much weather or lee helm. In which case you can try changing the rake of the mast. A yacht that has had it's mast removed and the re-stepped may well suffer from an increase in either lee or weather helm simply because the mast rake has been wrongly set.

But it's fairly easy to correct. Easing the forestay and tightening the backstays, making sure that the shrouds keep their correct tension, will move the rake of the mast aft and reduce lee helm by moving the centre of effort aft. You can try to reduce a permanent and excessive weather helm by easing the backstays and tensioning the forestay, thus moving the rake of the mast forward.

If you think that this more drastic action is needed, it might be sensible to ask a rigger for advice, rather than attempt this on your own. If you do it wrong, it's possible to introduce a bend or twist in the mast that won't be able to be corrected without major surgery on your wallet. Most yachts are designed for a specific rake and a specific range of sails, and a rigger will be able to correct any errors in both stay tension and mast rake.

Using the tides

On a long ocean passage and in the open ocean tides are not so much of an issue. But on a short passage in tidal waters, using the tidal strength and direction efficiently can get you into port before closing time. But there's one mistake that novice yachtsmen make, particularly in these days of electronic chart plotters, and that's trying to steer a straight line over the ground rather than through the water.

Only fight the tide when you have to

It's very tempting, if you're looking at the chart plotter and you see the yacht slowly being pushed to port or starboard of the plotted course over ground, to try to bring her back 'on course'. But you could be adding considerably to the length of your journey.

The example usually given to show this is a channel crossing from the Needles to Cherbourg. The passage is sixty nautical miles more or less, and at five knots it will take twelve hours - more or less one tide's worth of time. You are travelling more or less at right angles to the direction of the tide.

If the tide is running at, say, one and a half knots, and you start your passage at the turn of the tide, you'll spend the first six hours being taken at one and a half nautical miles per hour away from your course in one direction, ending up nine miles to one side or the other of your plotted track over the ground.

But for the following six hours, the tide will be bringing you back again at more or less the same speed, so by the time you reach Cherbourg, you'll be more or less back on your plotted course over the ground.

The experienced skipper will simply steer the course plotted (in this case, more or less 180 degrees true) and ignore the drift from the plotted COG, knowing that the tide will bring him back before he gets to Cherbourg.

The novice, however, will be watching the chart plotter like a hawk. He or she will see the yacht being swept away from the plotted COG, and will make course corrections to stay 'on the line'. This creates two problems: a slower passage because the yacht is fighting the tide all the way across, and a longer passage because more miles are sailed at a slower speed.

The key tidal issue with a passage to Cherbourg isn't maintaining the plotted COG, but ensuring that your course, whatever it is, leaves you up tide of the harbour entrance when you get there. The tides around the Cherbourg Peninsula are strong, and if you arrive down-tide of the entrance in a three knot tide and an adverse wind, it's entirely possible that you'll spend a good few hours looking at the harbour entrance as you make best speed but without being able to reach it!

In any waters where there's a significant tidal factor, and particularly in waters where the tidal flow is strong, it pays to do your tidal calculations carefully and to plot them. And if there's a significant wind shift en route, it pays to plot them again. The issue isn't where the tide is taking you 'now', but where the tide will put you in relation to your planned COG on arrival.

In fact in strong tidal waters, the tide direction and speed is often more significant than the wind. Rounding Land's End is a classic example. Land's End is a true tidal gate, but in addition to the six hours of favourable tide that you should be able to expect, you can also squeeze a further three and a half on a north bound passage by using the counter-current eddies that run close inshore. So if you plan to be in position off the Runnel Stone two hours before High Water Dover and keep within a quarter of a mile of the shore, you'll get a good tidal lift. If you're off Brisons at High Water Dover, the tide should then be good for another six or seven hours, and even a small yacht should be able to reach St. Ives with a reasonable wind in that time.

Remember that the tide will always flow faster in a deep water channel, so if you're caught out, use the depth sounder and charts to find shallower water. You might even benefit from a favourable back eddy.

Remember, though, that tides are rarely what the table or tidal diamond says they will be. They are 'predictions', and all sorts of factors will change the predicted set and speed of the tide. Strong winds, barometric pressure, heavy rain inland resulting in higher water in an estuary, and even minute variations in the orbit of the moon - all of these can change the predicted height, set and rate of tide.

If you've got an awkward bit of pilotage that relies on good tidal planning, one little trick is to find the outer marker buoy of the entrance, and stem the tide so as to hold your position off the buoy. After the yacht has settled down, you'll be able to read off the reciprocal of your heading which will give you the set, and you'll also be able to read off the speed (provided your electronic log is reasonably accurate). Compare that with the prediction, and you can make corrections if necessary.

Lee bowing and tidal planning

There's a lot of discussion about 'Lee Bowing'. The theory is that by sailing with the tide on the lee bow, the tide will free you up by a few degrees, giving you a better point into the wind. Some yachtsmen think it works. Others don't. My own view is that it might work for racing yachtsmen, where a few seconds gained can make the difference between winning and losing round the next mark, but for the average cruising yachtsman it's more trouble than it's worth.

I'm not going to repeat the arguments for and against here; there's plenty of discussion online and in print, and some racing yachtsmen use it all the time. There are experts on each side of the argument. My own experience is that it's much more sensible to use the tide to best effect for the overall passage than to try to construct a course that might give you a few minutes gain on one leg at the expense of a longer overall passage.

So I tend to ignore lee bowing completely. If the most efficient use of wind and tide happens to put the tide on the lee, then so be it. But as they say, correlation does not imply causation.

Balancing the Yacht

It might seem rather an obvious point, and it might seem a little distanced from traditional sailing skills, but it's worth thinking about the fore and aft balance of your yacht. If you have too much weight in the bow of the yacht, she'll be bow-heavy, and that will both slow you down and make you very wet in any kind of seaway. So it pays to think a bit about balancing the storage of heavy stuff like spare anchor chains, spare water, tins of food, etc.

Ideally the yacht should be trimmed so that she's slightly lighter in the bow than at the stern.

In a small, lightweight yacht, this can be a major issue. Getting your stowage right, and trying not to put too many heavy objects up forward, will help you gain a few tenths of a knot - not a lot on a short passage, but it can make a considerable difference on a long passage, and it can keep the helmsman and on deck crew a little dryer.

Anchoring

You will, no doubt, have covered all the theory about anchoring in your RYA courses. You may even have actually done some, though I'm not sure how often it's examined as part of the YachtMaster ticket. The art of good skippering isn't so much knowing how to anchor: we assume this knowledge when we take command. Rather, the art of good anchoring is in knowing 'where' to anchor.

Fairly obviously, you will need to anchor on the best holding available. But if that means you're crossing the anchor chain of your neighbour, you won't be popular. Just as you need your own personal space in order to feel comfortable with others, so too a yacht needs it's own 'personal' space, distanced from others. It's only polite to respect your neighbour's need for such personal space, and anchoring too close is one of the cardinal sins of poor skippering.

If there isn't room to anchor without coming a little too close to your neighbour, the very least you can do is to ask if he or she minds. Disgruntlement about the anchoring behaviour of other skippers is one of the most common complaints on forums and in yacht club bars. So please, do be considerate of your neighbour's need for personal space!

Heavy Weather

Whole books have been written on dealing with heavy weather in a sailing yacht, and it's not the purpose of this book to repeat them. If you're any kind of skipper you will already have read some of them. But it's worth touching on the main issues.

As I see it, dealing with heavy weather is a matter of working with two things. One is your sailing skill, the other is your fear.

If you've ever been in a real storm at sea you'll know that one of the unexpected things is the noise of it. The noise of the wind in the rigging is incredible. It doesn't howl, it screams. The crashing sound of the yacht hull hitting the water as it falls of a wave is bone-shaking. After a particularly nasty night in a force ten in Biscay, I heard the skipper ask no one in particular: 'Did you hear that crash last night? I thought the bow was coming off!" It was true. The yacht, a solidly built Hallberg-Rasy, had fallen off a wave in a particularly heavy way, and the noise was something I shall always remember. A Hallberg-Rasy is a particularly well-built long distance cruising yacht, and will take a lot more pounding than this. But the noise and slamming was incredible.

Fear is inevitable, and if controlled, is actually a healthy response to danger.

And with skill, sufficient distance from the coast, and the right tactics, most yachts will weather a storm at sea. What they won't weather is shallow water, breaking seas, rocks, or the poor decisions of a skipper who is paralysed by fear.

So, as I say, two things are needed.

Skill in dealing with heavy weather is firstly about changing your mind set. On passage, you're set on making distance. In heavy weather, you're set on safety and comfort. And often safety and comfort result from the same actions.

Having a heavy weather plan is all part of your preparation. It will depend in part on the characteristics of your yacht, and in part on your location and the nature of the storm. Being close to a lee shore in a gale may well require a different response from being well out to sea in an offshore gale with plenty of sea room to run.

Brief, secure, prepare

If you have warning of the approaching heavy weather, then you can start your plan. I have a three point plan which is: brief, secure, prepare.

The briefing is to let your crew know what to expect, to allocate jobs, and to deal with their fear or apprehension. Just as you don't want your own fear to cloud your judgment, neither do you want their fear to incapacitate them.

The management of fear requires one or more of three things. Either (a) assured safety, or (b) being in control, or (c) a means of escape. As Skipper, you have a reasonable assurance of safety and are in control, even if you don't have the option of a means of escape. But your crew has none of these. So you need to supply the deficit.

Brief

The first task in any storm briefing is to help your crew manage their fear. You can do this firstly by reassuring them about the sea keeping abilities of the yacht, and by any other ways that you think might help. After all, it's true that most yachts will survive a storm far better than their crew! This is 'the assurance of safety' that's so important.

Secondly, you can help them to feel more in control. Involving them in the preparation of the yacht, giving them specific jobs, and helping them to feel that their contribution will make a clear difference to the comfort and security of the team, will give them a measure of control and help them manage their fear.

Secure

The sea is a powerful force. Sea water weighs in at over one ton per cubic meter, and a few cubic meters washing up the decks or breaking over the bows can do a lot of damage. So the decks need to be cleared. Stow anything that can possibly be washed away, and if you can't stow it, then lash it down firmly. The decks need to be clear. Stow the dinghy. Stow the anchor. Seal up the hawse pipe with the chain on the end of a line so that it can be quickly recovered. Tape up the clips on the guardrail gates (they can easily be washed undone, and you don't want the steel lines flogging the clips against anything). Check the clips are secure on all lights, and if necessary, tape them up to show at a glance that they are locked closed.

In fact, follow your storm preparation check list. You do have one? If not, prepare one.

The same process needs to be done below. Nothing, and I mean nothing, should be loose in the cabin. All cooking equipment, all navigation equipment, and all personal belongings need to be stowed in a cupboard with catches that work. Having a pair of navigating dividers flying across the yacht in a storm isn't fun, and a loose pair of binoculars shoved into a cubby hole can become a guided missile when she falls awkwardly off a wave.

I've often been on yachts where some of the cupboard catches are loose and the cupboards need to be jammed shut with bits of card or paper. It's clumsy, irritating and a sign of poor seamanship in good weather. But in a storm its just plain dangerous. So if you find cupboards that don't close properly, sort them out before you meet heavy weather.

The same goes for all enclosures with a catch. On yachts fitted with a front-opening refrigerator or freezer, then sticky tape or gaffer tape can be used to tape them shut. Sticky tape is easily removed, but can help to alleviate the repeated stress on a fridge door catch that it was never designed to take.

Sort out your lee cloths and allocate each member of the crew to a bunk. Don't bother with the forward cabin - it will be too bumpy. If necessary, double up aft. Personal space is going to become even more personal in a storm, so don't be too twee about it.

Once again, and at the risk of irritating repetition, I find that having a storm preparation check list is a great help because I don't want to forget something vital when it comes to doing it for real.

Prepare

Storm sails need to be raised and, if possible, main sail and foresails removed and stowed (but see my hints and tips below). If the yacht can be made to heave to with storm sails set, then that's a great way of weathering out a storm. But a yacht that's likely to sail in seas where severe weather is a reasonable expectation can manage quite well with heavily reefed working sails if they are properly prepared.

Reefing hints and tips

Most main sails come with three reefing points. But even the third reef can leave you with far too much sail in very strong winds. It is both possible and prudent to get your sail maker to sew in a fourth set of reef points, leaving you with a fourth reef with the same sail area as a tri-sail. That way, provided your sails are strong, you don't have to fit an extra track for a tri-sail, or have the problem of removing one sail and rigging another.

It's the stitching in the sail that's most likely to degrade through ultraviolet

(UV) exposure, and strong winds will do the rest, often at a time when you're least able to deal with it. To mitigate this, you can ask your sail maker to put in four rows of stitching on each seam, and then sew on a cover to protect that stitching from chafe and UV exposure. That way your seams are less likely to degrade and split in a strong wind!

And whilst you're about it, ask your sail maker to add webbing handles at the luff of the sail so you or your crew can get a grip on the luff to pull it down quickly when reefing. Gravity isn't going to work in a storm, and trying to pull the sail down using the luff line or sliders is frustrating and a potential cause of broken fingers. The force on the luff line is considerable when it's blowing hard, and getting fingers trapped in the folds is a risk.

It's more than useful to have a reefing ring on either side of the sail. That way, you can always reef the mainsail from the windward side of the yacht. If you reef by sailing close to the wind and letting the main right out, and you've only got one reefing ring on the leeward side, you're putting yourself or your crew in a very dangerous place.

In my experience, the easiest and most useful reefing system is a separate tack line and clew line, rather than a single line system. Single line reefing systems are heavy and easy to jam, particularly when the winds are strong. And a reefing ring on both sides of the sail is essential, so that you can reef on the windward side no matter what tack you are on.

Try to practice lowering the sail and taking in the reefing lines at the same time to avoid them flogging and tangling. A well-practiced reefing is a joy to behold, particularly in heavy weather. And if it's well practiced, then it's a lot safer for everyone, because no one likes going on deck in heavy weather (and the skipper won't like it much either if it all goes wrong).

Avoid mainsail in-mast furling like the plague that it is. It might be fine for gentle sailing in warm waters and on large yacht with electric winches and uniformed crew, but it's heavy to use, ruins the shape of the sail, and is the easiest reefing system in the world to jam. If you reef the sail in a hurry and at the wrong tension or position, you're likely to put creases into the main that are almost impossible to remove without a trip to the sail loft and surgery on your wallet.

And if you're sailing in seas where heavy weather is likely, then pay attention to the cut of the foresail. You don't need the clews right down to the deck. They, or their attendant sheets, can snag on things. Clews at deck level make it difficult to see forward. Ask your sail maker to cut the foresail with high cut clews. That has three major advantages. Firstly, potential snagging is avoided. Secondly, visibility forward is hugely improved. And thirdly, the sail shape when reefed down hard is a lot better. If your sails are conservatively cut with hollow leeches, then you will be well placed if you don't want to change down to storm sails. You can simply adopt your heavy weather reefing positions.

Drogues and trailing lines

A lot has been written by many well-respected skippers about the deployment of drogues, lines, or other paraphernalia over the stern of the yacht in a storm. The purpose of these is to slow the yacht so that she doesn't sail faster than the run of the sea and end up pitch poling. But deploying drogues or long lines is a difficult and dangerous business. The strain on the attachment points can be horrendous, repeatedly putting the full weight of the yacht on them. Would you try to lift your yacht out of the water using the cleats, the davits or the stay attachments? Or worse, would you allow someone to bounce her on them? Even with purpose-built attachment points, the stresses are horrific. And if one of the attachment points pulls out, you have an immediate ingress point for water.

Recovering them after a storm is even worse. Anyone who has ever tried to haul in a drogue that's been fully deployed will tell you the same story. It takes ages, is hugely difficult, and puts a dreadful stress on the crew. If for any reason you need to make a quick getaway, you're faced with the only option of cutting the lines or drogue adrift. They cost money, and good ones are hard to cut away without a hacksaw.

It's much better to set up the yacht so that she is heaved-to, or so that she lays a-hull. You're not interested in making distance during these conditions, and the comfort and safety of the yacht will be much higher this way. In fact, a well set up yacht with plenty of sea room that is heaved-to in a storm can be pretty much left to her own devices, whilst the crew is safe and warm below. Try it in moderate weather. If you've not done it before, I promise that you will be pleasantly surprised at how the motion and noise are both eased.

Food needs to be prepared - soup in a thermos, secured properly. Sandwiches. Snack bars. Water. All of these need to be to hand but well stowed. And part of the preparation is to make sure the crew is well fed and watered before the storm hits you.

Weather it

Once the storm hits, and if you're properly prepared with the yacht heaved-to or lying a-hull with plenty of sea room, then you can all retire below to your bunks. The watch system needs to be maintained, and if possible (or necessary) the track of the yacht marked on the chart every few hours. But in the worst storms, watch keeping can only realistically be done from shelter. Putting your crew into the worst of the weather when there isn't much they can do isn't really wise.

Once the storm is passed, the yacht is likely to be a mess. People may have been sick, gear may have shifted, and boxes and bottles may have broken or opened. Clearing up takes time, but it's worth spending a day or so getting things back to normal.

There are many books written on managing a yacht in bad weather, and I can only briefly touch on it here. But these three things I think are at the heart of your storm plan:

1. Have a storm preparation check list along with a storm plan for the yacht. A lot of the preparation can be done before the yacht leaves harbour. Pay attention to sails, and practice, practice, practice. Above all, practice reefing down to your storm reef.

2. Make sure your mind set moves from making distance to maximising safety and comfort. That way you won't be tempted to push on and overstress the yacht and the crew.

3. Brief, secure and prepare the yacht. Your crew are likely to be nervous, if not outright frightened by the prospect of a storm. Briefing and giving them jobs will help a great deal.

STEP SIX - KNOWING YOUR YACHT

If you don't know your yacht, you're in trouble! So before you slip lines, you need to make sure that you know at least the key systems of rigging, steering, engine, battery management, communications and domestics. And that you not only know them, but can deal with each of them if they give you problems.

A story to get us started

It's four o'clock in the morning, there's at least 28 knots of wind, a nasty seaway, heavy rain, you are three hundred miles from the nearest land, and you've been asleep for only an hour after a long watch. The on-watch crew, who happens to be the first mate, shakes you awake to tell you that there's a major water ingress, and it's already up to the cabin sole. You step out of your bunk into half an inch of water. The lights are already out because water is over the batteries and they are shorted. Which means that the heavy-duty bilge pump isn't going to work either because it needs electricity.

Your first action is to taste the water. If it's salty, it's sea water. If it's not, then it's likely that the large fresh water tanks have failed and it's probably not an emergency. Unfortunately, the water is distinctly salty. Your instinctive action is to stop the engine in case a hose has failed and it's pumping raw cooling water into the yacht rather than out of it.

Having done that, what are your priorities?

I'd suggest that there are four of them in the following order:

1. To let someone know your position and the nature of your difficulty.

2. To prepare for evacuation to the life raft if you can't stop the ingress.

3. To locate the ingress and to try to stop it, or at least slow it down
4. To pump like there's no tomorrow.

You're not going to be able to do all of these yourself, so you'll have to delegate. You have a compliment of three crew, one first mate and yourself. You tell the first mate to get the remaining crew up and into life jackets, and to instruct two of them to get the life raft out of the lazarette and tied on ready for deployment, and the other to start pumping. The life raft crew are to prepare a supply of water and food, to locate and ready the grab bag, but they are NOT to launch until or unless you give the command.

Once he's done that, the first mate can start looking for the point of ingress. You tell him that you will use the Satellite phone to alert Falmouth MRCC of your problem, and you will then join him in the hunt for the leak.

You have instructed the crew to keep an hourly written log, so the loss of electricity or even your back up GPS won't mean you are completely lost. You get the latest position from the log whilst you switch on your hand held GPS. Once MRCC have been informed of your approximate position, the number of people on board, and the nature of the distress, they will probably instruct you to keep them informed every half hour, and to let them know if you have to abandon ship. Meanwhile they will start the process of diverting a nearby ship to come to your aid.

The three crew members are busy getting the life raft ready, and you quickly check that they have it tied onto a strong point ready for deployment. That's all that matters for now - the rest they can take care of themselves.

Your job now is to coordinate the hunt for the water ingress. The first mate confirms that there was no impact of which he was aware. So the most likely points of ingress are either one of the through-hull fittings, the prop shaft, or the rudder stock.

As part of your safety brief, you asked each crew-member to draw a plan of the yacht, noting the position of each of the through hull fittings. You asked them to check that each one was fitted with the correct grade of hose, that it was serviceable and secured with two jubilee clips, and that the valve was operational. You then got them to show you where they were, and to demonstrate that the valves were not corroded or stuck. You also got them to point out where the wooden bungs were kept, along with the hammer or mallet for knocking them into place.

Or did you?

Practice for all kinds of emergencies

I've taught hundreds of students to do a 'man overboard' exercise at the start of a passage, so that the crew know exactly what to do if I, or one of them, go overboard. It's an important part of the RYA syllabus. In fact, I almost failed my Yacht Master Coastal many moons ago because I didn't pick up under sail, but used the quick stop method (which at that time was a fairly new procedure and involves the engine). The RYA are very hot on practicing MOBs.

But there are other emergencies besides MOBs that can and should be practiced. I've had a fire on board a motor-sailor at four in the morning somewhere between Kefalonia and Messina. At first it seemed like an electrical fire and we treated it as such, but it turned out to be an engine room fire.

A similar procedure needed to be followed. I had to delegate one crew to shut down all generators including the wind generator and then ready the life raft. I had to get a Pan Pan off quickly in case we lost electrical power. The first mate didn't have to be asked to find and deal with the fire!

But I really did need to know where things were in the dark without having to look for them. Knowing your yacht can make the difference between staying afloat and having to take to the life raft.

Let's get back to our hypothetical water ingress.

The life raft is ready to go, the grab bag is ready, and one of the crew is already pumping the hand pump. The others grab a bucket each and start getting rid of water. With a major water ingress, speed is essential, and you don't want to have to start trying to find through hull fittings in the dark, especially as they will by now be under water. You should know exactly where they are and how to reach them.

All the through-hull fittings seem to be OK, but just to be sure, you close each one off after you've checked it. Which leaves the rudder stock and the prop shaft. The first mate makes for the steering bay under the aft lazarette, and you take the engine covers off. You see that there isn't a prop shaft any more. In fact, there's a considerable ingress of water through the stern gland bearing where the missing prop shaft should be. You've found your water ingress, and your hand makes a very good temporary bung!

You call the first mate back and shout for the bungs and the hammer. The one remaining problem is how to get enough force behind the hammer in such a cramped space, under several inches of water, to drive the bung in firmly. But for now, the tapered wooden bung is in the hole, and the ingress of water is all but stopped.

You can relax a bit, and the crew working with pump and buckets can pace themselves. You've now got plenty of time to get the yacht dried out, the bung firmly and properly secured, and the situation under control.

It's time to put the kettle on, call MRCC Falmouth to let them know you've located and stopped the ingress of water, and relax a bit. You have sails, and even though you can't start the engine with the dead batteries, you can easily sail to the nearest port for repairs, monitoring the temporary bung like a hawk!

Of course, it's a fictional account. And I've written all of this at my desk a good few miles from any yacht. But I've based it on my own experience of problems at sea, including water ingress from an unknown source. And the point of saying this is that you too can play a 'what if' game on various emergencies to try to learn both how to cope with them, and to make any changes that might give you a better chance of getting home safely.

One immediate question is whether you should have stopped the engine. Without batteries, you can't re-start it. Sure, it might be pumping sea water into the yacht, but it might also be useful if you can divert the intake from the impeller to the flood water so that the engine can help you pump out. What would you have done?

These kind of 'what if' games are very useful, and can help you not only prepare for possible emergencies, but also help you improve your yacht and your skippering skills. As an example, let's see how many lessons we can learn (in no particular order) from this fictitious 'water ingress' story. Here are the more obvious ones:

1. Knowing the location and condition of every through hull fitting by heart so that you and each member of your crew can find them, close them (with bungs if necessary), and deal with any problems in a seaway and in the dark. This includes the rudder stock and the stern gland where appropriate.

2. Having fully charged torches to hand and ready for use.

3. Trying to ensure that your batteries are as well protected as possible from water ingress. This might mean re-locating them, or constructing some kind of protection for them. They should already be placed in a leak-proof box to prevent spilled acid from leaking out and corroding important fittings. Sealing them inside the yacht is not a good idea because if they gas, they need to be able to vent. But locating electrical connections as high as possible can help buy you time.

4. Practicing crew jobs in various potential emergency situations so that every crew member knows his or her job and does it without confusion or having to be asked.

5. Possibly having a spare battery, fully charged, well away from any

potential water ingress so that you have a spare 'just in case'.

6. Keeping a hand-held GPS near the chart table, and some spare batteries nearby, so that you can always fix your position if your power fails.

7. Ensuring that your crew keeps an hourly running log of at least position, course and speed and marks the chart, so that if all else fails, you can quickly estimate your position by dead reckoning.

8. Making sure that the life raft and grab bag are not hidden at the bottom of a locker under loads of other gear.

9. Thinking about emergency communication, and having a communication plan. In this case, satellite phone was an option, but what if you don't have one? Can you jury rig power for the vhf or ssb?

10. And do you have enough buckets?

Maybe there's more. Perhaps the biggest question is how the prop shaft came to detach from its universal joint. You might think this a little too far fetched as an example, but it is based on a real event. The prop shaft was held into the universal coupling behind the gear box with grub screws. With a feathering prop turning the gearbox for many hundreds of miles, the shaft worked loose and the whole shaft including the prop came adrift.

Which brings us to maintenance.

Knowing your yacht's key systems

The yacht's systems can be reduced to a number of key units. Standing rigging, running rigging, steering, engine, anchor, navigation, communications, water, fuel, domestics, and so on. Don't forget the anchor as a discrete system: like the brakes and handbrake on a car, it's one of your key safety systems.

Trying to devise an inspection and maintenance plan for the whole yacht is a daunting task when you also have the running of the yacht to manage and possibly watches to stand as well. But you can reduce the task, and even make it manageable, by dealing with it system by system. The most important ones are the ones that will get you back to a safe port, so standing rigging, running rigging, sails and steering are key. Engine follows, then communication, water, and so on.

I once brought a yacht from Marseille to Corfu, and the day after we arrived in Corfu, I took one of the owners out for a lesson on planned navigation under sail. As I left the marina, I noticed that there was a little slack in the wheel steering. As the lesson progressed, so did the play in the steering. I stopped the yacht, opened up the inspection covers, and checked the steering wires. Sure enough, one had come off it's pulley system, frayed, and was only connecting by a couple of strands. We very gently sailed back to the marina, and I learned an important lesson. Even on a long passage, systems need to be checked regularly. If that wire had broken on passage, we may have been forced to use the emergency steering. And all because I hadn't checked the steering during the passage. It's easy enough to adjust the tension on the steering links, but once the wire is frayed or broken, it's the devil's own job to re-do it at sea.

Most leisure yachts are designed with the weekend yachtsman in mind. A long passage can create considerable wear and tear on the many different systems, particularly those that flex and move regularly like running rigging, steering and sails.

Create an inspection routine

So it's important on a long passage to create and maintain some form of regular inspection routine for the various different systems. You could create an elaborate set of paper checklists and keep them with the logbook. You might invest in computer based planned maintenance software like 'A ShipShape Sailboat' and run it on your laptop at sea and in harbour. A more portable version for the iPad is My Boat. Or you could simply note systems headings and dates checked in the logbook, running through the systems in your head as you work through them. But however you do it, you need to do it. Things wear out and break, and if it happens in bad weather or just as you're navigating the Chenal du Four, life will quickly become very interesting indeed.

Don't be afraid to dig around in the guts of the yacht to trace a system through properly. It's all too easy to neglect something because it's too much bother moving kit. Steering is a good example, because on a wheel steering yacht it's often a set of wire cables running through pulleys, attached to chains and set up to move an armature or some other link to turn the rudder stock, with the whole shebang well hidden and buried in the deepest darkness of the yacht.

Part of the system may be buried under the lazarette bottom board. Inspection will involve emptying the lazarette of odd lines, fishing gear, dinghy, oars, boat hooks and all the paraphernalia that gets shoved out of sight, pulling out the bottom board, and performing a contortionist act to get at each moving part. Some of it will be inside the wheel post, and will require you to remove at least one inspection plate with screws that may not have been unscrewed for half a lifetime. Shrug your shoulders, skip the difficult bits, and you could well find yourself without steering on some dark, wet night. It probably hasn't been checked, let alone greased, for years.

My own routine is part plan, part intuition. I like to take one system a day, and walk through it, getting to know it thoroughly. If I have questions, I check the maker's website online, read the manual, or ask others. I may even 'phone a friend. But the harsh realities of modern sailing yacht fittings with their built-in tendency to fail at the most inconvenient times has taught me not to skimp on these checks. Even if it means delaying a departure for a couple of days or annoying the crew, who have to cope with fitting everything back into a lazarette that's somehow shrunk in size since the dinghy was taken out.

Another simple, but important check is on the gas line. Tracing the line from the gas bottle through to the cooker can be another contortionist's dream, but if you find chafe, you may well have saved a very nasty 'accident' from happening.

At the front of your mind as you walk through each system are the two questions 'How can this go wrong?' and 'What would I need in order to fix it?' Each little bit of each system needs to be checked with these in mind. Whether such an approach would have prevented our hypothetical prop shaft separating from the gearbox is an open question; it's often only after the event that you kick yourself for overlooking some aspect of a system check. But if you don't do the checks, the dice are much more heavily loaded against you.

The problem with all but the highest quality yachts built for extended long distance cruising is that most of the equipment is fitted with the weekend sailor in mind. It's fine for someone who day sails from a marina and whose extended passage making is for a two week summer holiday. But on the average leisure yacht the equipment and fittings are not often designed for extended periods of continuous heavy use. So a long distance passage on one of these is inevitably going to throw up equipment and rigging failures. As a skipper, you need to be aware of it and to prepare for it. Having the right basic tools and spares is one part of the equation. The other is being self-reliant in basic repairs and maintenance, and being ready to jury fix something if necessary.

A commercial endorsement will require you complete a sea survival course: what to do if the yacht sinks. It will require at least a basic level of first aid. Fire fighting might be part of an extended training programme. Whilst these are clearly important, from my own experience of delivering all kinds of yachts, there are three other key things I'd recommend:

1. An extended diesel engine maintenance course that really gets your

hands dirty changing bits, replacing impellers, filters, and bleeding fuel lines, together with a thorough understanding of how the different kinds of marine diesels work. And every time you get on board a different yacht as skipper, get your hands dirty checking how to do it, using the yacht's toolbox. A missing spanner might mean you can't bleed the fuel line. A missing wrench might mean you can't change a fuel filter.

2. Time spent with a rigger going over the rigging on at least one yacht. I learned so much from a few hours with a rigger that I was able to spot a potential issue with a furling foresail on one yacht that would have lost us the forestay, and possibly the mast. Standing rigging is the framework for getting the best from the sails. Knowing how it works, how it is tensioned, and what to do if you suspect it is slack, or broken, or about to break, is a key skill.

3. A thorough grounding in how batteries work, how they are charged, and how they deliver their volts and amps to the various bits on the yacht that need them. Electrical systems are a mystery to many weekend yachtsmen, and as a result they tend to get neglected, run down, or simply wired up wrongly. People tend to add bits, forgetting to amend the wiring diagram (if there is one - how many yachts do know where you can immediately turn up the wiring diagram to trace a fault?). The result can be anything from a nasty smell from an overheated battery box at some inconvenient moment, or a slow and steady loss of amps from important navigational equipment, to a spectacular fireworks display followed by an electrical fire.

As skipper, you will need to take responsibility for all of this. Stuff happens at sea, and if it happens to you and you don't know how to deal with it, then you may well be in trouble.

Knowing your yacht is firstly a matter of knowing the various systems on board. We've already seen how you can break these down into manageable bits. But there's more to it than just understanding systems.

Planned Maintenance

There's a lot of maintenance that you can do yourself. A combination of experience and planned learning will enable you to do most things in time. Changing an impeller, a fan belt, or a fuel filter are probably the most basic tasks, along with a sail repair kit and a few hours practice at sewing canvas.

But there are some essential tasks that you will need to contract out. These don't usually need to be done every year, but they do need to be done. And chief amongst these are a rigging check and the life raft service.

Rigging Check

I'm constantly amazed at the way some people put their yachts up for sale with poor rigging, out of date life rafts, rusted jubilee clips on worn out hoses, and so on. But what amazes me more is that other people buy these yachts without challenging the vendor about them. Just because the mast is standing up doesn't mean it will stay standing up when the yacht falls off a wave in a strong seaway. And just because the rigging looks 'OK' to an untrained eye doesn't mean it hasn't got serious faults that will cost a lot of money to repair or replace.

The majority of rig failures stem from a failure of either the lower or the upper terminal fittings. A visual check can reveal the tell-tale signs of rust or a broken strand at the top of a swaged terminal. Running your fingernail over the terminal itself can reveal cracks that the eye would strain to see. Checking the alignment of the chain plate with the shroud is another simple test. If it's out of alignment, then something is clearly wrong, and the chain plate may be seriously weakened.

Galvanic corrosion on the mast, loose or corroded rivets, or a corroded mast step can all be signs of more serious problems.

If you have any suspicion about the condition of the standing rigging, it pays to ask a professional rigger to inspect it and give you a report. Or better still, spend time with the rigger on board. You'll learn a lot more than just whether the mast is about to fall down.

Standing rigging can last a lot longer than many insurance companies' estimate of ten years. But somewhere between ten and fifteen years on the average white boat is the time to replace it. How often you do this is up to you, but I wouldn't leave it more than three years before I get a rigger on board, and a lot sooner if I've got any suspicions.

Looking after your standing rigging is hugely important. The cost of replacing shrouds is going to be a lot less than recovery at sea and a complete new mast and boom.

Liferaft Service

The other key inspection is the life raft. Again, I'm amazed at how often I'm asked if we really need a life raft. It shows an almost complete ignorance of the nature of ocean or coastal sailing. 'We've got a dinghy' is the standard defensive reply when I ask whether they can swim thirty miles in icy sea water. But the dinghy just isn't equipped to look after you in an emergency. If I'm taking command of a yacht, one of the questions I'll ask even before joining is whether the life raft is in date. If it's not, then it's a show stopper until it's serviced.

I once spent a week on a club yacht, a very nice if somewhat elderly Oyster, off the west coast of France. On the safety tour of the yacht, I asked to look at the life raft. It had been due for service at the beginning of the year, and was clearly out of date. Yet the club was sending between six and eight people each week to sea on that yacht. When I asked why that happened, the answer was that 'they thought it was probably good for another year'. That kind of thinking causes serious accidents. If they were willing to play with the lives of their members, then it's not a club I wanted to join.

If you've got to deploy the life raft, the one thing you don't want to be thinking is that it will 'probably' work. And you certainly don't want to be explaining to the Marine Accident Investigation Board why you put to sea with the life raft out of date. It's the skipper who is in charge, not the club officers or the charter company. And if that skipper is you, it's down to you to make the call. I've had to do it on three occasions, and on each one the owner considered me a pedant. That's one of the things you learn when you take command: to take responsibility even when people think you're wrong.

If you don't want the expense of buying and maintaining your own life raft, you can hire one. The hire company will make sure that the thing is in date and is properly serviced. On a recent delivery from Crete, I had a hired life raft flown out. Yes, it cost a bit more because it had to be classified as 'dangerous goods' (because of the flares and the compressed CO_2) but the hire company was excellent, arranging all the paperwork. I arrived in Crete, went to the airport, paid my 40 Euros for the privilege, and walked away with a brand new, in date life raft. It cost the owner a lot less than buying one and servicing it.

Getting the life raft serviced when you have left European waters (or even in some European jurisdictions) can be difficult. But again, planning will take care of it. If you know when the service is due, it can be part of your planned maintenance.

If you can afford the time, be present when the life raft is serviced. Examine it when they inflate it. Look at what's in the survival pack (if there is one). See how it all works and how it all fits together. Like being with the rigger, you'll learn a lot more than the mere fact that the life raft is good for another few years.

Knowing your yacht's behaviour

All of the yacht's systems work together to give each yacht its own characteristic behaviour. It will sail in a certain way, heave to in a certain way, go backwards in its own distinctive style, and lie at anchor in its own fashion.

No one, even if he or she is a brilliant skipper, is going to know these characteristics without trying them out. You might have a good idea, based on experience, of how a particular yacht will behave. A heavy long-keeler isn't going to go backwards under engine in a marina in any predictable or even safe way - lines might be needed. A gaff rigger isn't going to sail too close to the wind. A bilge keel will give you bucket loads of leeway if you over canvass her too close to the wind. In fact, you might even be able to sail her sideways. And so on. But knowing your yacht is more than just knowing the systems that make her what she is.

For example, a furling headsail will often affect how close she will sail to the wind on each tack. On port tack she might sail a good five or even ten degrees closer than on starboard, especially if you're sailing with some of the sail rolled away. This is because what should be a knife-edge, or at least a knife handle edge, has become a pillar with the sail on one side of it. It will cut the wind much better on the tack where the pillar of furled sail is behind the leading edge, rather than in front of it. Knowing which is the better tack can gain you considerable time over a long distance.

So it pays to practice. I was once delivering a heavy displacement centre cockpit yacht from Spain to the UK, and we needed to find shelter. The marina was narrow, cramped, and almost full, but there was one space we could use. It was a horrible afternoon with strong winds. The drawback was that we would have to reverse into the one vacant space on a sharp right angle because if things went wrong, we would need to go forwards fairly quickly to avoid being blown onto rocks. And if for any reason we lost way, she'd be blown straight onto them.

So I sat outside the marina entrance in the bay and practiced in at least a force seven. We must have looked quite idiotic from the shore, motoring backwards and forwards outside the marina entrance in that weather. But the result was an almost perfect execution of a difficult bit of boat handling, the safe arrival of the yacht in its berth, and the confounding of the ghouls who had gathered on the marina to watch a yacht piling up on the rocks.

If you want to know how the yacht will handle under different conditions, then practice. Try it out. Find some sheltered bit of water somewhere where there aren't any lumps of rock or other shipping, and practice. And don't forget to give your first mate and crew a chance to practice as well. You're all learning, and you never know when you might want your crew to do it for you.

Important domestic systems

It's not just the boat handling characteristics that you need to know. Knowing how the water system works will help you plan water use for the passage, but that's not much use if you don't monitor water usage. And if there's an electrically powered pressurised water system on board, always, always check that you have alternate ways of accessing fresh water. An electrical failure can deprive you and your crew of fresh water if you don't have some means other than the electric pump of getting at it. An additional foot pump or manual pump at the sink is a very good idea.

Knowing your electronic kit

And you need to be able to master the navigational kit. Some makes are more intuitive than others. Personally, I love the Raymarine kit, and offer a silent cheer if it's fitted to a yacht I have to deliver. Putting a floating EBL (Electronic Bearing Line) on a radar display to keep a safe distance off shallows, or setting a range alarm, seems so instinctive. There are some makes that seem to go out of their way to hide important functions deep inside a menu system. The first mate and I once spent a whole passage from Southampton to Liverpool trying to figure out how to remove waypoints from a particularly esoteric chart plotter. The manual was in Japanese. At least, I think it was Japanese. It might just as well have been English, because even when we had located and English version of the manual online and downloaded it, we were none the wiser.

It takes time

All these are important, and you'll be a very highly skilled skipper if you can master them on the first day out. Which is why a shake down sail along the coast in good weather before setting off across an ocean is important. It not only gives time for faults to reveal themselves, but it also gives you time to learn the various systems on the yacht.

One of the reasons I stopped teaching for sea schools was because of the pressure to go to sea on a Friday evening with an inexperienced crew who didn't know each other, who didn't know the yacht, and who were tired after a week's work and a long drive. They were supposed to be sailing the same evening as they arrived on board. I managed to get some idea of their experience and competence before we left, but I'd much rather have spent a quiet evening on board going through the yacht systems with them before setting out to sea. Being thrown in at the deep end may work as a rather crass way of sinking or swimming, but it's risky when it comes to sailing a yacht.

Using your ears

You're not going to be able to monitor everything all the time. If you're not watch keeping, you need to eat, sleep, relax and switch off. But the one thing you can do is to attune your ears to the sound of the yacht.

I learned this very early on. I was sailing with a very good friend of mine who is now a YachtMaster Instructor, but who at the time was simply a good leisure skipper. We were on passage, and I was on watch. He suddenly put his head up through the hatch and said that I'd better stop and check the impeller. He was right. The impeller had disintegrated, and the cooling water had stopped. His ear was highly attuned to the sound of the engine, and he picked up the subtle change in engine note that resulted from the failure. There was an overheat alarm on the engine, but his ear picked up the problem before the temperature had time to rise enough to trigger the alarm.

It works with sails as well. Listening to the sound of the yacht on various points of sail will tell you a lot about how she's sailing. Very often, less noise is better. A properly tuned rig will send the yacht through the water in the most efficient way. Wind noise in the rigging, or a flogging leech, or even an uneven creaking, can tell you a lot. And sometimes your ears can pick up danger and send an alarm to your brain when the rest of your senses are completely relaxed. If your sixth sense begins to ring an alarm bell, check it out. It may well be your subconscious reacting to a change in the sound of the yacht.

I was once sailing south a good fifty miles or so off the Portuguese coast. It was a glorious day with the wind on the stern quarter, and I was off watch and reading a book in the cockpit. I'd casually spotted a trawler on the horizon, a good five miles away, noted it's relative bearing, and checked that the watch-keeper had seen it. Happy, I went back to my reading. Because we had the wind almost fully aft, I'd rigged a preventer to avoid accidents with crash jibes, and the yacht was set up for a long downwind passage.

I noticed the watch-keeper go below to fill in the hourly log, and went back to my reading. But my ears were awake, and after about three minutes they sent an alarm to my brain. I could hear the sound of a large diesel engine. And it sounded close. I looked up to see the same trawler bearing down on us at about fifteen knots only a few hundred yards away, no one visible on the bridge. There wasn't time to unrig the preventer, and the only way to avoid a collision was for me to grab the wheel, disengage the auto-helm, and crash jibe around the stern of the trawler, backing the main and putting massive strain on the preventer gear. Amazingly, the preventer held, stretching a bit, and so did the standing rigging, and we went into a kind of reversed heave to with the main backed and the foresail drawing. We skittered around the stern of the trawler and I'm not sure who was more surprised - our watch-keeper below or the trawler crew stowing kit on the aft of their fishing vessel.

A failure to monitor the movement of the trawler was entirely our fault - she was showing the usual fishing cones, even though she was clearly not fishing - and it was my ears, rather than my eyes, that prevented a nasty collision.

It's tempting to spend all of your off watch time reading and relaxing. But it's more profitable to spend at least some of that time learning the yacht's systems, learning how she behaves, learning how things work. Reading the manuals is often the last resort of a frustrated operator, but an hour or two spent with the file holding the manuals to all the yacht's systems can be really helpful.

Each yacht is different. From the brand new yacht delivered to the marina for the first time to the yacht that's been round the world a couple of times and is showing her age, each one will have its own quirks, its own faults, and its own advantages. A new yacht is no more likely to sail without problems than an older yacht that's been well used. In fact, in my experience, a new yacht is much more likely to throw up issues. Getting to know your yacht inside out and back to front is one of the key tasks of a safe, professional yacht skipper.

STEP SEVEN - KNOWING YOUR RESOURCES

All of the skills in the previous steps are necessary. But these are necessarily focused on the individual passage. In order to be a great skipper, you also need to be aware of the issues, trends and developments in the yachting world as a whole, and as far as possible keep up to date with the many developments in leisure yachting.

This means being aware of the huge range of resources available today for the sail cruising skipper.

Joining an organisation like the Cruising Association or the RYA is helpful, as is reading widely in the yachting press and online magazines. If you're anything like the average Skipper, you'll be doing this already because of your continuing interest in the world of yachting.

Knowing yourself

And of course, you are the greatest resource you have, so it's a good place to start this chapter. One of the key skills in being a good skipper is knowing your own strengths, your weaknesses, your ambitions and your limits. For most of us, insight is a long and sometimes painful journey. But you won't have arrived at the point of skippering a yacht without having learned some difficult lessons on the way. Draw on those lessons.

Learn from your mistakes

I learned. I learned from my mistakes and my successes. I learned that I love the seas, the oceans, and the quiet solitudes of the night watches. I learned that I am not good at detailed planning and need to work at it. I learned that I sit light to bureaucracy. I learned that I am light on crew briefing and need to ensure that I communicate efficiently. I also learned that I am very good at getting a yacht to sea, and sailing her to a destination port.

And we all have our 'confessionals', those stories about embarrassing or dangerous moments that could have been avoided. Maybe they are best kept to ourselves, mulled over, and used as personal learning. Sharing them can be amusing, but once out, it's often difficult to put the cat back in the bag!

A Skipper who has finished learning is a Skipper who should have finished sailing. To enlarge on a famous quote by Oliver Wendell Holmes (1841 - 1935):

> *"I don't give a fig for simplicity on this side of complexity, nor do I care much for complexity the other side of simplicity, but I would give my very life for the simplicity on the other side of complexity."*

The point being made is that there is usually a process through which we travel in order to get experience. At first, we simplify things in order to understand the outline shapes and contours of the problem. But sooner or later that simplicity gives way to a much greater complexity as we try to absorb the large amounts of detail necessary for a proper understanding of the problem. However, if we stick with it for long enough, there comes a point at which the many complexities resolve themselves into a kind of simplicity that sees the important things and knows the detail without having to look it up all the time. Skippers who have reached this kind of simplicity radiate a kind of quiet confidence born entirely of knowledge, understanding and experience.

So where are the places that a good skipper can continue to learn once he or she is at sea with his or her own command?

Reading MAIB reports

They may not be your idea of bedtime reading, but one of the most fruitful ways to learn from other people's mistakes is by reading some of the recent MAIB reports on serious marine accidents. The Marine Accident and Investigation Branch is the maritime equivalent of the Air Accident Investigation Branch. Set up after the Herald of Free Enterprise disaster, the MAIB investigates maritime accidents to British flagged vessels, particularly where people have lost their lives, in order to help others learn from mistakes, identify weaknesses, and avoid further incidents.

The level of detail, combined with the forensic analysis of the events and issues contributing to the incidents, make these reports a real aid in developing professionalism as a yacht skipper. The MAIB has a section for leisure craft, and it really does pay to read the reports. They are detailed, thorough and highly professional accounts that seek to help mariners to learn from the mistakes of others. As their website states:

"The sole objective of the investigation of an accident under the Merchant Shipping (Accident Reporting and Investigation) Regulations 2005 shall be the prevention of future accidents through the ascertainment of its causes and circumstances. It shall not be the purpose of an investigation to determine liability nor, except so far as is necessary to achieve its objective, to apportion blame."

As an example, it's worth reading the report on the fatal Man Overboard from the sailing yacht 'Lion', not least because it was the skipper himself who lost his life.

A 'man overboard' is one of a skipper's worst nightmares, and I've had cause on a number of occasions to warn even fairly experienced members of my crew about the risks of both inappropriately adjusted lifejackets and the use of life lines.

The report raises yet again the debate about using life lines, or 'tethers', as the report calls them, and underlines the need for both long and short 'tethers'. A life-line is only any use if it stops you falling overboard. If you end up in the sea, attached to a yacht travelling at more than half a knot or so, the pressure of sea water on your body can be so great that you can't take any action yourself, even if your face is in the water. You end up pinned, often against the side of the yacht, and you can easily drown.

In this case, the problem was made worse because there is some doubt about whether the crotch straps on the skipper's lifejacket were properly adjusted or even attached. I am continually surprised by the number of crew who have never been taught how to wear and adjust a life jacket properly, or shown the risks of the jacket riding up over the wearer's face and head if the crotch strap is not used, or not correctly adjusted.

The report states:

> "In an emergency, whether it is a fire, flood or a man overboard situation, effective and coordinated incident management is of the utmost importance. Strong leadership, good communications and an unequivocal understanding by the crew of who is in charge are key factors to ensuring a successful and safe outcome." (Para 2:8)

The full report can be found on the MAIB website at http://www.maib.gov.uk/cms_resources.cfm?file=/Lion.pdf.

Reading these reports will help you in two specific ways.

Firstly, they will help you recognise a specific danger or risk when you are at sea. Most incidents are not caused by one single isolated event. They are most often the result of a chain of events where things go progressively wrong. These may or may not be connected, and by themselves they may appear minor, but put together they can contribute to a very nasty outcome.

A good Skipper will recognise such a chain starting to form. Even recognising just one of these events and stopping it may prevent such a chain leading to a nasty 'accident', but the risk is that you might appear to be somewhat pedantic to an inexperienced crew. But remember what I said early on: you're not there to be liked.

As an example, I was once en route from Pireus to Kefalonia at night. Against my instructions, a crew member had decided to put all of the spare fuel in the reserve fuel can into the main fuel tank because he didn't want to have to do it in a seaway. At first, that might have seemed to be common sense, but it struck me at the time as a foolish act that could, if combined with other factors, lead to a nasty incident.

What if, off the rocky coast of Kefalonia, we had had a fuel leak and lost fuel from the tank, or my fuel calculation had been wrong and we had run out of fuel? What if this had been combined with one of those Mediterranean calms and a drift towards rocks? We would probably have had time to drop the anchor, but that coast is very steep to, and it's unlikely the anchor would have found bottom to hold us before we were on the rocks. Maybe we would have had time to call for some more fuel or a tow. But needing extra fuel, or a tow, in such circumstances could be construed as 'salvage', at great cost to the owner. And what if the tow wasn't available?

The job of the skipper is to think of these 'what if's'. Reading the MAIB reports will help you develop the kind of sixth sense the might just prevent a chain of events building up to a major incident.

At one o'clock in the morning, sailing without any reserve fuel began to play on my mind. I went through the usual 'what if's', and decided to return to Piraeus to refuel and restock the spare fuel can. It will have seemed to the crew like a pedantic act (and I got more than a few grumbles from the owner who was on board at the time), but I would rather be seen as a pedant than take unnecessary risks with the yacht and the crew.

Secondly, reading the detail and professionalism of these reports will help you to develop your own professionalism and your own eye for detail. Little things like checking that the crew members know how to wear and properly adjust a life jacket, and how to manage a life line so that it's short enough to prevent you going over the side, become important because they are important, not because you are unnecessarily picky.

Of course, if you are too cautious you'll never leave the marina. But there's a real difference between developing a personal culture of safety and being so scared of the risks that you don't put to sea. The MAIB spend many thousands of pounds employing highly professional and experienced mariners to produce these reports specifically so that people like you and me can learn from them. So it's worth your time reading them.

Talk with other skippers

Socialising is part of the fun of sailing, and inviting other skippers on board for a sun-downer or a fish supper is a great way to expand not only your social circle, but also your experience and knowledge. Inevitably, when two or more skippers get together, there will be tales told of adventures at sea. Keeping your inner ear open for opportunities to learn what went wrong, or encouraging an honest appraisal of a tricky situation can be a great way to learn.

And sailing with another skipper is simply a variation on this. Sometimes I sail as first mate with a skipper I have known for a long time and who I respect considerably. I will always obey the chain of command, but that doesn't mean that I sail uncritically. If there's something I don't understand, then once the passage is complete, I will ask about it. That way I continue to learn.

Using sailing forums

One of the problems with online sailing forums is that there are a large number of armchair yachtsmen who use them, and not all the advice given there is either useful or safe. But they can be a great place to get a second or third opinion on an issue, or to gain help with a passage plan from people who have sailed it before.

One of the more useful sailing forums is the private forum run by the Cruising Association (C.A.). It's only available to members who have to use their real names, and public cross posting is not allowed, which means that the amount of bad tempered stupidities found on other forums are largely absent. It's one of the main reasons I know for joining the C.A. Whilst the forums run by the major sailing magazines are very variable in their quality (and the members can sometimes be rude to the point of obnoxious, which simply emphasises their inexperience), the Cruising Association forum is populated by people who are active yachtsmen and women, and who are actually doing the sailing that others on the more open forums just dream about.

Sail planning websites

Sailing websites are another place to go for information. We've already mentioned http://www.noonsite.com, (see Step 2) which is perhaps the leading website for ocean yachtsmen planning their visits to other countries and possibly my favourite yachting website. But there is a whole raft of sites that are useful for planning.

In case you've not already met them, here are the top four of my favourites:

Noonsite. As already mentioned, this is the 'must read' website for any yachtsman visiting a new country or a foreign port. The information is solid, accurate, and a fine addition to the paper pilot books available for most waters.

ECMWF is the European Meteorological Office website and gives medium term weather forecasts for all parts of the world. In a conversation with one of the UK Meteorological Office staff, it emerged that ECMWF is the model that the UK bases its forecasts on. It's a 'must visit' before setting off on any offshore passage, and it's free.

Mediterranean Wave Forecast. Published by the Israel Marine Data Centre, this website includes a really useful forecast for wave height in the Mediterranean. Novice yachtsmen think of the Mediterranean as an idyllic calm blue sea with wonderful sunshine, great ports, and fascinating history. It is all of these. But it can produce some of the nastiest seas anywhere in the world. Some of those seas can often be found South East and South West of Crete, as well as in the Western Mediterranean south of Marseille. It's another 'must visit' before setting off on a Mediterranean passage, and it's also free.

Admiralty EasyTide. Published by the UK's Hydrographic Office, this site gives free tidal predictions for the next six days, but you can subscribe and get predictions well into the foreseeable future. It saves having to carry tide tables about, but as we've said earlier, paper doesn't rely on an electricity supply for its information, so it's always best to carry essential navigation tables and charts with you in paper or book form.

iPhone and Android Apps

The rise of the tablet and the iPhone has seen a large number of Applications (or Apps) developed for the leisure yachting market. It was a good few years ago, shortly after the first iPhone was introduced, that I first met the world of Apps. I was teaching a Day Skipper course and one of the students proudly showed me his new iPhone complete with charts of the Solent and the South Coast.

Being a traditional yachtsman, and wanting to emphasise the importance of running an hourly plot on paper charts, I was a little dismissive of the concept. But a good few years later, going into Argostoli in Kephalonia at one o'clock in the morning, I had my 'epiphany' experience.

We were entering using the rather sparse lights (the Chart Plotter had failed for some reason), and had just done the double back turning using the single white light on the promontory. I was tired, having sailed all the way from Corinth in one hop, and it was a pitch black night. Those who know Argostoli will know that there are a couple of important green lights that need to be accurately identified, and I got completely confused, not sure which one I was looking at. The depth started reducing rather dramatically, and there was only one option and that was to turn around and start the entry again. I gave the bad news to the on-watch crew.

But one of the off-watch crew then placed his iPad in front of me. He had equipped it with iSailor and the charts of the Mediterranean (at a ridiculously low cost). As the iPad was equipped with a GPS receiver, it showed me at a glance exactly where I was, and immediately resolved the confusion. I was able to re-orientate myself on the right green, and actually ended up using the iPad to enter and moor stern-to on the lovely, if shallow, town quay.

When I asked him how much the charts cost, I was stunned. For something under twenty pounds, he had equipped himself with charts for the whole of the Greek waters. A further small sum had given him charts for the rest of the Mediterranean. They looked accurate when compared with the Admiralty charts we were carrying, and with each Admiralty chart costing in the region of twenty pounds new, they were an absolute bargain.

So one of my first actions on returning to the UK was to buy an iPad and equip it with a number of yachting apps. iSailor remains my first choice for electronic charts, but I've also added a number of others. Here's a short selection of my favourites:

iSailor by Transas. Not only one of the cheapest ways to buy accurate electronic charts, but also increasingly becoming an alternative to the chart plotter, as it gives other data as well. There are others, and it's a matter of personal preference, but mine is iSailor.

Pocket Grib. A simple grip display that allows you to download grib wind forecast charts for the area in which you are sailing. Small, useful, and takes up little memory.

Tides Planner by Tubaco. Like the Admiralty app, but better in my view. Gives you tidal flow charts as well.

Boatie from MoJoSo. A kind of all round 'Swiss Penknife' app for yachtsmen. Navigation, weather, tides, and a host of reference stuff that makes the first section of Reeds a little redundant.

My Boat by Intelligent Maintenance. This is a great planned maintenance and inventory app that's well worth the £12 cost. It makes planned maintenance a breeze, and is worth the money simply for the ability to create and maintain an on board inventory of spares.

Anchor Watch. Does what it says. But I'm a traditional yachtsman and if there's any risk of dragging, I prefer a person to an app for Anchor Watch.

POST SCRIPT

I hope that reading this little book will have helped you in some small way to develop your skills as a safe, competent and engaging skipper. It may well be that over time the book will be added to and expanded. That's one of the joys of publishing today.

If you'd like to keep up with any developments and changes, then please visit our website, www.7stepbooks.com, and sign up for the updates.

And if you'd like to comment on anything you've read, there's an email address on the website that will reach us.

Thank you for reading.

APPENDIX 1 - CREW INVITATION FORM

This crew invitation form is included for you to adapt or use in whatever way suits you. Having some form of joining instructions and a kit list is always helpful, and together with the personal information section, should be the minimum you send. The remaining information can be used, or not, as you see fit.

Dear John,

Joining Instructions – Passage from Gosport to Gibraltar

Following our conversation on the telephone recently, I am pleased to invite you to crew for us on the following passage:

Vessel Name:	YachtName
Departure port:	Haslar Marina, Gosport, UK
Destination port:	Gibraltar, UK
Joining Date:	28th July 2014

Estimated duration of voyage: Estimated 21 days, but may be shorter.

Travel and costs contribution: We will pay agreed cost of return flight to UK Airport from Gibraltar on completion. We will ask for a financial contribution of £50 per crew member towards food. drink is not provided but you are welcome to bring your own provided you are willing to share it!

Your Skipper will be:	Joe Bloggs, YachtMaster Ocean Instructor
Address:	Skipper's address

Telephone:	Skipper's telephone
Email:	Skipper's email

A very warm welcome to the crew team. I trust you will have a very enjoyable voyage. Our overriding aim is to sail the yacht safely, expeditiously and in the best possible condition to its destination. But we also want all crew members to enjoy the voyage and have the best possible experience of crewing.

Please complete the crew information form, sign to say you have agreed the crew conditions, and return a copy to SKIPPER NAME (returning the signed document is sufficient to show agreement) before departure and in time for him to answer any specific questions or issues. Returning this invitation is your agreement to make the voyage and you will not be able to make the voyage without doing so.

Please contact SKIPPER NAME for detailed instructions for joining. All we know at this point is that the yacht is likely to be in Haslar Marina, but SKIPPER NAME will have the full details.

If you have any questions relating to the transfer or the voyage, please don't hesitate to telephone me. My contact details are: contact details here.

I look forward to welcoming you on board and I wish you a very enjoyable voyage.

Skipper's name here

Crew Information

Full Name as it appears on your passport:

Passport Number:

Passport Issuing Authority & Nationality:

Your date of Birth:

Contact telephone number:

Your home address:

Your next of kin (or someone we can contact in an emergency):

Address:

Telephone:

Your RYA or other relevant qualifications (you may be asked for proof of these):

Do you have any medical conditions that your skipper should be aware of? If so, please state them here, together with a list of any medication that you take. Please remember to bring all required medication with you.

Do you have any special needs or diet requirements?

Kit List.

Please ensure that you include the following in your kit. Please call if you have questions:

Foul Weather suit	Gloves
Harness & Safety Line	Inflatable Life Jacket
Sea Boots	Deck Shoes
Warm head gear	Sleeping Bag
Passport	Torch and batteries or wind up torch
Adequate personal funds	

Crew Agreement

The following conditions are not designed to be unduly restrictive, but to make sure that everyone understands the nature of the invitation to crew, to avoid unnecessary confusion, and to enable the skipper to manage the passage to the highest standards of quality and professionalism. They are designed to ensure the safety of all crew members and to enable you and your colleagues to have the very best sailing experience. If you have any questions, please contact the skipper at the earliest opportunity. His task includes creating the best possible sailing experience for crew members.

Please read the following, and sign to say you understand and agree:

1. Your position on the vessel is on a voluntary basis and does not create an employer/employee relationship.

2. The voyage is not a commercial voyage, and the requirements of the Maritime Labour Convention 2006 do not apply. However, we will keep to the spirit of the convention with regard to the well being of our crew.

3. You will be over 18 years of age on the day of joining the vessel.

(If you leave this out, then put something in about Parental consent and Child Protection, and whether the child will be required to stand night watches, or indeed any other work at all!)

4. The Skipper is lawfully in command of the vessel and its crew at all times. You must undertake all duties required of you by the skipper, and obey all lawful requests for the duration of the voyage.

5. Sailing is a relatively safe activity, but there are risks and although the Skipper will do his best to ensure your safety neither he or anyone else can be held liable for any loss or damage to your property or personal possessions, or injury or death, however caused. Crew must take responsibility for their own safety and have adequate insurance. We will ensure that there is a culture where all safety issues can be openly discussed onboard. If you have any concerns over your safety or the safety of the vessel, please discuss them with your skipper.

6. Delays en route can occur for weather, technical or other reasons. In the event of delays, whatever the cause, we will discuss and agree options with you. Please do NOT book return flights before arrival at the destination port because if we are delayed or end up in a different port, the flight could be wasted.

7. In the event of scheduling or routing delays we will not be responsible for any associated costs incurred by you. We advise you to take out travel insurance for these risks.

8. The voyage will be 'all found' within an agreed budget. Within this budget, you will not have to pay for any food or non-alcoholic drink on board. You will be given your agreed travel contribution by the Skipper on disembarkation at the port of delivery. A sum of £50 per crew member is requested towards the food kitty. You are responsible for all your own living costs and any other expenditure when not aboard the vessel.

9. You may be given time off during the voyage when in any port at the discretion of the skipper, but will be required to be back on board, able to crew, at the time stated by the skipper.

10. The Skipper's standing orders will be found in the Log Book, and will cover such things as the wearing of life jackets, safety procedures, watch keeping, and other routine but necessary operations to ensure a safe passage. You will be asked to sign the log book saying that you have read

and understood the standing orders before sailing.

11. You must bring your own personal safety and other equipment, which must include at the very least a Coastal Foul Weather suit, sea boots, gloves and head gear, lifejacket, harness and safety line and sleeping bag. You must also provide yourself with at least two changes of warm clothing, a torch and batteries (or wind up torch), and adequate personal funds. If you have any difficulty with any of these, please contact your skipper who may be able to help.

12. You will not bring on board any drugs, weapons, publications or other material proscribed by UK, EU, and other relevant jurisdictions. If your skipper has any concerns about this, you may be asked to submit your belongings and person to search or inspection. If you are found to be, or suspected of being, in breach of these terms it may result in your immediate dismissal from the vessel.

13. Smoking on board the vessel or in its immediate vicinity is forbidden at all times. The consumption of alcohol whilst on board the vessel is forbidden at all times without the explicit and specific agreement of the skipper on each and every occasion. If you are found to be, or suspected of being, in breach of these terms it may result in your immediate dismissal from the vessel.

14. Should you leave or be dismissed from the vessel at any point en route you will be responsible for your own repatriation costs and all related expenditure.

15. You must notify the skipper of any current, chronic or recurring medical condition and of the appropriate medication / treatment. You must also inform the skipper on joining the vessel of any treatment that should be administered in the event of an occurrence of any medical condition. You are responsible for your own medical requirements, treatment and costs, including repatriation if necessary. You must hold your own medical and travel insurance and for voyages within the EU you should also obtain a European Health Insurance Card.

16. Unless otherwise agreed in writing you are responsible for all your own ground travel costs. Any agreement relating to travel costs will be nullified if you are dismissed from the vessel or leave the vessel for any reason before completion of the delivery.

17. You are responsible for ensuring that you have the necessary passport, visa and immunisation documents for the voyage.

18. All documents referred to in this agreement, and any certificates of qualification, must be provided on request for inspection by the Skipper, or

the authorities of the countries whose waters the vessel may pass through. You are responsible for operating within the constraints of your qualifications.

19. When you arrive at the final destination you will be asked to help with the cleaning of the vessel and any other maintenance work. You will normally be expected to leave the vessel within 24 hours or arrival at the final destination.

20. You may not at any time make any statement to the press or other form of public media about any aspect of the passage, both during its duration and at any subsequent time, without the written consent and approval of the Skipper.

I have read and agree the terms above.

Signed: ....

Date: ....

Please print your name: ....

APPENDIX 2 - EXAMPLE OF STANDING ORDERS

The following standing orders are usually attached to the Log Book, and crew members are asked to read them, and to sign the log book saying that they have read and understood them. On occasions, I may decide to send them along with the joining form. These are an example of the kind of thing that might be useful to include, rather than a definitive list. You will have your own ideas about what should, and should not, be included.

Standing Orders

On duty watch keepers are to wear Life Jackets at all times when at sea and if watch keeping in harbour.

Off duty watch keepers are to wear Life Jackets above deck at sea unless the skipper has given specific permission for 'relaxed routine'.

Relaxed routine will be noted in the log, along with the resumption of normal working routine.

If you need to go on deck (i.e., out of the cockpit) whilst at sea, only do so with someone else in the cockpit. At night or in rough weather, both must be clipped on.

Ensure you know and follow the Collision Regulations. If in doubt, refer to the copy kept in the chart table and improve your knowledge of them!

If a ship is approaching on a steady bearing, and you are uncertain what to do, call the skipper BEFORE it reaches 3 miles.

Sail changes require three crew – two on deck and one in the cockpit.

Mast climbing requires three crew. One to climb (taking VHF handheld), one on main winch line, one on safety line. Do NOT attempt to climb the mast on your own.

If you have a PLB or strobe, note the details in the log.

As far as humanly possible, we will maintain a blame-free culture where mistakes are there to learn from, and where all of us, including the skipper, can learn from each other. Do not be afraid to challenge the actions of any other crew member, including the skipper, if you think something is dangerous or wrong.

Watch keepers

The safety of the yacht and its crew depend on you during your watch.

Relieve the outgoing watch at least 5 minutes before the hour to allow for a thorough handover.

Keep a good lookout at all times, and regularly check behind you for approaching shipping.

Maintain the log every hour on the hour whilst at sea, and mark the chart with position and time.

Check the bilge at the start of your watch and record details in the log.

Always keep at least 5 miles to seaward of any coastline or outlying danger. If you need to approach closer than 5 miles, call the skipper and obtain permission before doing so.

Use active AIS whenever possible. In rough weather, always use active AIS.

Pots and Nets. Keep a good lookout for pots and nets, even at considerable distance from the coast. Long (over five miles) unmarked drift nets are a real concern in the Mediterranean at any distance from the coast, and long nets should be expected within 20 miles of the coast. If you spot a marker buoy, check for others in line with it. At night, a small stationary radar echo may well indicate a pot or net marker. Check for parallel movement with floating EBL if possible.

1600 – 2000 watch keeper to check the battery levels at the start of your watch, and run the engine to charge if necessary, so as to avoid running the engines during the night watches if possible. However, it is important to maintain enough amps to run the radar and AIS during the hours of darkness.

If in doubt or concerned about ANY aspect of the passage, call the skipper.

Night routine – between Sunset and Sunrise

Clip on whilst in the cockpit. Do not go on deck without another person in the cockpit, when both of you will be clipped on.

AIS: Ensure that the AIS is running and active between Sunset and Sunrise.

RADAR: It is not necessary to run the radar continuously at night when traffic is light (it can take a lot of AMPs), but as a minimum check radar for traffic using at least three sweeps every 20 minutes. If a contact is within 8 miles, run continuously, and ensure you have plotted a CPA using either the EBL to check for steady bearing or floating EBL on wakes, and continue to plot until it is past and clear. DO NOT GUESS. If in doubt, call the Skipper. Do NOT trust MARPA to give you a CPA.

Check shipping navigation and other lights using the Binoculars.

Fog Routine

Call the skipper if fog occurs during your watch.

Note your position, course and speed in the log.

Ensure that the AIS and the Radar are running.

Check radar thoroughly for contacts, and plot any to ensure a safe CPA.

If sailing fast, reduce speed by slackening sails.

All crew don Life Jackets

Make sure that the engine key is in, and that the engine is ready to run at a moment's notice. Warm it up if necessary. Only start the engine if necessary to ensure enough Amps for the Radar, but stop the engine to listen every fifteen minutes, or to a routine agreed by the skipper.

Make sure the fog horn is to hand. The signal for a yacht in fog is the Morse Code 'D' (One long, two short).

Man Overboard.

Call all hands immediately. Shout 'MAN OVERBOARD' loudly.

Crash Stop the yacht, without losing sight of the casualty (heave too).

Do NOT loose sight of the casualty. Point at him.

Throw over the Dan Buoy and / or ANYTHING else that floats and can mark the sea area.

First crew responder will:

- Use the MOB button on the Chart Plotter
- Mark the position in the log and on the chart

Second responder will:

- Take over the spotting and do nothing else

The Skipper (or Mate, if the Skipper is overboard) will take charge of the rescue.

Aim to bring casualty to the side of the yacht and secure by best means.

Recover the casualty by any means possible, including launching a tethered liferaft if recovery is difficult. We WILL practice and there MAY be exercise MOBs during the passage.

Fire

Call all hands immediately by shouting FIRE FIRE.

All hands to don lifejackets and muster in cockpit

Mate plus one to form fire attack party.

Skipper to take over watch and make any necessary Pan Pan call to alert authorities of the situation.

Cockpit crew to ready the liferaft, but NOT to launch without skipper's explicit order.

Response speed is of the essence.

ABOUT THE AUTHOR

Richard Thomas is a commercially endorsed Ocean Yacht Master, holds an RYA Instructor's ticket, and has been a Yacht Delivery Skipper for some years. He runs a yacht delivery company called 'YachtMovers' (http://www.yachtmovers.co.uk)

He has instructed for a number of UK Sailing Schools. Before he started his Yacht Delivery business, he was Chief Skipper for European Yacht Charters Ltd., running a Lagoon Catamaran for clients, and before that he spent four years in the Royal Navy.

Richard has considerable experience skippering many types of sailing yacht in the UK and the Mediterranean. He has heavy weather experience in Biscay, has dealt with a fire at sea, with numerous rig and mechanical breakdowns, and with several dangerous incidents. All have ended well.

In addition to his sea-going experience, Richard is a member of the Chartered Institute of Public Relations, a PR Consultant with the Public Relations Consultants Association, and runs his own communications business, Spider Communication Limited.

YACHTMOVERS
european & worldwide yacht deliveries

We'll help you move your yacht out there ...
or bring her safely home again

Our experienced RYA Instructor skippers can come with you to help you move your yacht to a new cruising base. Its a great way to learn.

Or we can provide a complete crew to bring her home again. We're members of the Cruising Association too.

Save both time and money.
Call or email us to discuss the issues first.

www.yachtmovers.co.uk

info@yachtmovers.co.uk
+44 (0)7919 017835

Printed in Poland
by Amazon Fulfillment
Poland Sp. z o.o., Wrocław